TRACKS ON CANVAS

The railway paintings of **PHILIP D. HAWKINS**

A wonderfully evocative scene at the west end of Platform 1 at New Street in April 1957 – the year that Villa won the cup! The gallery of spotters is perched on the engineers department window sill and many are wearing their school caps. A Monument Lane tank, No. 40118, busies itself with station pilot duties and signalbox No. 5 can be seen in the background. (Author's collection)

TRACKS ON CANVAS

The railway paintings of **PHILIP D. HAWKINS**

Dedication
For Nina and Ben

This edition published in 2009 by Heathfield Railway Publications
A division of Eagle Editions Ltd
11 Heathfield
Royston
Herts, SG8 5BW
United Kingdom

Copyright © 1998 Philip Hawkins
First published 1998 Oxford Publishing Co

ISBN: 978-1-906974-00-8

HRP.TOC

Acknowledgements

Thanks are due to the following who have allowed access to paintings in their collections: David Antley Esq, Bernard Apps Esq, Roy Apps Esq, Mike Armstrong Esq, David Asbury Esq, Gordon Barker Esq, Mr & Mrs D. Barrie, Ron & Freda Cass, Mrs 'Tot' Clarke, Paul Freer Esq, Andrew Harper Esq, John Hobbs Esq, Ron King Esq, Richard Martin Esq, Charles Pagett Esq, Eric Pearce Esq, John Petcher Esq, David Reynolds Esq, Bob Robson Esq, John Stockton-Wood Esq, Colin Washbourne Esq, Richard Willcox Esq.

And to the following organisations for their permission: BBC Radio Devon, Bristol United Press Ltd, Brown & Root, Booz . Allen Ltd, European Passenger Services, Midland Independent Newspapers Ltd, The Royal Mail.

Grateful thanks also to WBP of Birmingham who photographed many of the paintings for this book, Eversheds of Kingston upon Hull, Barry Everitt Associates, Simon Elvin Ltd, Quicksilver Publishing and many other organisations who have seen fit to make use of my work over the years.

Special thanks to Nigel Harris for his foreword and to Bernard Apps and Nick Pigott for their 'appreciations'.

Very special thanks to June Holloway for miraculously converting my scribble into pages of type.

The following paintings reproduced in this book are available as Fine Art prints from Quicksilver Publishing, 'The Sidings', 52 Teignmouth Road, Teignmouth, Devon, TQ14 8UT.

The Midlander, New Street 1957, On Time, Night Wolf, Waiting in the Night, Night Call, Night Freight, Island Summer, Evercreech Junction, Duchess of the Night, Firth of Forth, St Pancras Departure, East Coast Elegance, The Power and the Glory, Sunshine and Steam, The Bristolian, Unsung Hero (Ltd Edition), Twilight of the Fifties, Twilight of the Twenties, North Pole Dawn.

Contents

An Appreciation from Bernard Apps, Quicksilver Publishing

Being the Publisher of Philip's work is the culmination of a sequence of crossed paths that go right back to childhood. We were born within one year of each other in Birmingham, attended the same primary and grammar schools, but above all, our mutual love of railways was nurtured whilst trainspotting at the same place, where the former Great Western and LMS railways crossed at the bottom of our road in Handsworth. We both remember being lulled into sleep by the nocturnal sounds of the railway – sweet memories!

All of these coincidences came to light when, in my early twenties, I went into an off-licence in Solihull only to see 'railway paintings for sale'. The standard of the work amazed me. Here was an artist who actually captured the atmosphere of the railway accurately with the engines exactly as I remembered them. It was of course the early work of Philip Hawkins and I went on to purchase my first original oil painting.

I lost contact with Philip for ten years or so until we bumped into each other again, but this time I was now an experienced businessman and Philip was rapidly emerging as a leading professional artist. One thing lead to another and it was a natural joining of complimentary skills which resulted in the very successful Quicksilver Publishing, which we intend to see grow in the coming years.

Philip is a down to earth, very professional artist whose work never ceases to amaze me. He is in my view the leading railway artist in the country and the pictures in this book reflect his great talent. It is a privilege to have been asked to write this short testimony for Philip who is a great artist and a good friend.

An Appreciation from Nick Pigott, Editor, Railway Magazine

Tucked away in a corner of Philip Hawkins's studio is a small print depicting one of the celebrated Venetian masterpieces of J. M. W. Turner.

At first glance it seems a trifle incongruous hanging from a wall dominated by locomotive subjects. But to the owner of the studio, it is an inspiration – a constant reminder that rail art can count among its exponents one of the greatest masters who ever lived.

For Turner's *Rain, Steam and Speed*, a brilliantly impressionistic rendering of the then newly-opened Great Western Railway in 1843, helped initiate a genre whose popularity has grown dramatically in the succeeding century and a half.

Today, Philip Hawkins is one of a small body of specialised artists successfully perpetuating that genre for the benefit and pleasure of tens of thousands of railway enthusiasts.

Pleasing rail enthusiasts, however, is no simple task. A remarkably high percentage are perfectionists and wherever two or more are gathered together, a debate on railway art can be guaranteed to produce a lively and often heated exchange!

For the majority, the more esoteric aspects of painting such as surrealism, cubism and post-impressionism can safely be consigned to the realms of academia. Of far greater importance are such issues as the shade of the livery, the size of the tender logo and the shape of the driving wheels.

For locomotives whose wheels appear to be falling off the track, smokebox numberplates affixed at infuriating angles and physically impossible smoke effects are anathema to any self-respecting railfan. If just one such point has been badly executed – no matter how trivial the matter may appear to a non-enthusiast – the rest of the picture might just as well not have been painted.

The number of artists who fall foul of such criticisms is surprisingly high... yet full-time professionals such as Phil Hawkins have to please these armchair critics month in, month out if they are to earn a crust.

I first became aware of Phil's work when I was working in Fleet Street and keeping a watching brief on the enthusiast press in the late 1970s. At that time he was just in the process of turning professional and I remember making a note of his name as someone to keep an eye on in the future.

I have to admit here that where railway art is concerned, I am as pernickety and punctilious as any railway pedant and I can recall searching in vain for errors of detail or perspective in his work and, somewhat perversely, feeling cheated when I couldn't find any.

Phil's uncanny aptitude for somehow combining the accuracy of a photograph with the vitally-important 'look' of a painting impressed me greatly and has continued to do so ever since.

Much of the reason for his success, I later discovered, is the amount of time he spends researching his subject in the most meticulous and fastidious detail before brush is even allowed to touch canvas. For like all good enthusiasts, Phil himself is a perfectionist.

The results speak for themselves. Ownership of a Hawkins original is now a symbol of status in the railway world and after undertaking hundreds of commissions, he has yet to come across a dissatisfied customer.

Art is of course highly subjective and although one man's meat is another man's poison, Philip Hawkins' elevation to the Presidency of the Guild of Railway Artists proves he also has the hard-earned respect of his peers.

I am sure this collection of his paintings will give tremendous fascination, inspiration and happiness to his many admirers.

Foreword

I've always had great respect for those lucky folk who can take up pencil, charcoal or paintbrush and create pictures – but I'm especially impressed by those uniquely gifted individuals whose work not only convinces the eye but which stirs the soul, too.

For therein lies the difference between technical drawing and the finest art, which captivates for ever. An exaggeration? No – look in the world's art galleries and you'll find proof, for great art outlives us all. It continues to communicate for as long as it survives – and not just skills in perspective or technique either, but much more importantly, the artist's passion and appreciation for the subject.

I must take care, for I'm in danger of doing my friend Phil Hawkins a disservice, because even those of us with a satirical sense of humour run the risk of sounding pretentious when discussing art. We've all heard plummy critics (and, sometimes, even artists themselves!) spouting endless high-blown nonsense – but you certainly won't find Phil in their company, because his exceptional artistic talent is exceeded only by his healthy disregard for what he once described to me as 'arty claptrap!'

Despite Phil's talent in turning a blank canvas into memories which thousands of folk both share and relate to, he's a modest chap and tends to change the subject if you praise his work, which as this book shows is both extensive in range and of the very highest quality. He's worked hard to raise artistic standards in railway art generally and I've always admired his leadership of the Guild of Railway Artists which has played an important part in developing and improving all kinds of railway art. Phil was a founder member of the GRA and leads from the front with his steady output – so whilst I've known Phil's paintings for many years, it came as a surprise to me in this book that he's as creatively successful with a pen as he is with a paintbrush.

Just as Phil's paintings powerfully evoke 'the way it was', so his words had me chuckling along with him. For I too grew up in an industrial town of cobbled streets and small backyards and I too was a regular at the Saturday morning *Odeon* picture shows – for me, it was sixpence to get in, leaving around a 'bob' from my 1s 6d pocket money for some *Spanish Gold* confectionery

'tobacco' and a Lyons Maid *Zoom* ice lolly in the interval. Happy days! I laughed out loud at his tale of hordes of Saturday afternoon would-be Brummie 'Zorros', annoying the neighbours ("Go and play near your own house…!!") and leaping from advertising hoardings, gaberdine 'macs' buttoned around their necks as makeshift capes!

Phil powerfully evokes his childhood in early '50s Britain, when a word to your parents about you from the local 'bobby' earned you a clout first and questions later. This was the Indian Summer of the England of Enid Blyton – secondary school lads still went to school in short trousers, cars were required to 'Halt at major road ahead', AA patrolmen saluted members – and a squat glass jar of *Brylcreem* and an apprenticeship were the rites of passage into manhood!

And that's why Phil Hawkins is such a very special railway artist. He's not just a lucky chap who can draw and happens to paint trains. Phil really is 'one of us' – he's *lived* a good deal of what he paints and this is the magic ingredient alongside the burnt ochre on his pallette.

And I really do mean that Phil has lived what he paints – because the words in this book not only connect many of the locomotives and locations in his pictures with his own experience, but you'll also find the young Hawkins himself, together with members of his family, in some of the paintings. Family groups in old snapshots have been incorporated into his work to breathe a very special kind of life into his paintings. This book is a personal, very effective autobiography of a boisterous young lad of the early '50s, who doubtless sketched the spectacle before him at New Street when he wasn't 'copping' what he describes as 'the mechanical heroes strutting before him'. Wonderful stuff.

Phil is fascinated by the railway of earlier years which he wasn't privileged to see. His crimson 'Compound leaving St Pancras' (page 61) is a special favourite of mine – what amazing days they must have been and powerful pictures like this give us a taste of what it was like. There are lots more paintings I find myself returning to again and again: the country railway feel of E*vercreech Junction* (page 48) is delightful: the thrilling anticipation of *Duchess of the Night* is powerful (page 53) and the driver on the left, collar up, billy-can in hand and quite unmoved by the spectacle, is a wonderful touch. The cold

in *Western Blizzard* (the hunched, miserable shoulders of the flagman say it all!) is chillingly conveyed. This is a book to savour – repeatedly.

It's fashionable today to heap scorn on those who take an interest in railway, as being 'sad' and in need of 'a life'. I've always believed that my interest in railways was the stage on which I acted out my own formative years and learned to handle the grown-up world on my own two feet. 'Spotting' trips were my first tentative experiences away from protective parental control – and learning to 'sink or swim' in the wider world as served by the railway has stood me in very good stead. I'm glad I did it – and Phil makes the same point; that his interest in railways linked his other boyhood activities from acting out 'Zorro' to football and cricket. Each interest nourished the other to create a wealth of experience from which he now draws not just inspiration, but also 'feel', atmosphere and emotion.

And he's still hungry for new experience – where in the '50s it was New Street and Tyseley, it's now North Pole Junction and the 'East End' for Eurostar and the Docklands Light Railway – taking in Class 50s, Class 20s and Merry-go-round coal trains on the way. Truly, if it's on rails, it's likely to spring from Phil's palette – and you can be sure that the finished canvas will appeal to both eye *and* heart. It was a pleasure and a privilege to work with Phil on the *Unsung Hero* painting (page 89) produced in association with a *Steam Railway* appeal to raise the £70,000 needed to restore the National Railway Museum's Robinson Class O4 2-8-0 No. 63601, at the Great Central Railway – and Phil's involvement helped to push our final total well past our target, to more than £75,000.

As Phil Hawkins' work continues to mature, I firmly believe that he will be increasingly – and deservedly – acknowledged as Britain's finest railway artist.

But I bet you'll never find him guilty of 'arty claptrap!'

Nigel Harris,
Managing Editor;
*RAIL, Steam Railway,
Steam World, Model Rail.*
Emap Apex Railways Division,
Peterborough, Cambridgeshire.
May 1998

Introduction

For the last 20 years I have earned a living, of sorts, from my paintings which have been, with very few exceptions, of railway subjects. Practically all have been published in one form or another but never before in a book devoted entirely to my work. During the preparation I have received a great deal of advice and assistance from my editor, Peter Nicholson, editorial director Darryl Reach, and Alison Roelich, editorial department manager. My thanks are due not least for believing in my work but also for allowing my ideas and suggestions to reach fruition.

The paintings in these pages date from 1982 and cover a selection of work covering 15 years. Working drawings, sketches, pages from notebooks and photographs are included where appropriate which will, I hope, help to explain something of the thought processes which culminate in the finished article. The brief autobiography may help to explain the background and motives which drive me on, the writing of which has proved a fascinating and thought provoking exercise.

Although painting, and other art forms for that matter, tends to be a solitary process one of the delights of my career has been the help and encouragement received from many kind souls over the years. Some of these are mentioned in these pages, others such as Dick Potts, a great character and an ex Tyseley and Saltley footplateman, have been a veritable mine of information and anecdotes of real day-to-day life on Britain's railways. Their help has been invaluable and has helped lift otherwise inpenetrable black clouds on many occasions. My wife, Sonya, also a professional artist but not of railway subjects (thank goodness) has developed an effective line in backside kicking and honest, incisive critisism when apathy or despair threaten to take over. Nina and Ben, my children, now in their twenties, can also be relied upon for their veracity. Both, incidently, have appeared in my paintings, although not in recent years; Ben, for example, can be found in at least three pictures in this collection. These are salutary influences in what can sometimes be a fawning, deferential profession, and not always well received but invariably accurate.

The Guild of Railway Artists has proved to be a great source of encouragement. Meeting and talking with kindred spirits, sharing problems and solutions, receiving and offering constructive critisism. To have served as President since 1988 has been a great honour. Frank Hodges, the Guild's Chief Executive and founder deserves a very large medal!

Much of my work is commissioned, both private and commercial. These range from vague requests to the most highly detailed specifications. Meeting and discussing a prospective painting with these brave souls and discovering their reasons is fascinating and results in subjects and locations that otherwise would not be considered. Sometimes a discussion will span many meetings and involve copious amounts of photographs and general reference, other times the briefest of chats will suffice. Either way I prefer quite an amount of input, particularly regarding composition, lighting and angles etc, and have declined work where I have been unable to achieve this.

Those with scant knowledge of painting and indeed art in general often imagine that it all happens as if by magic, a simple clicking of the fingers perhaps, but as with most professions, hard graft, knowledge, practice and years of experience with the odd splash of that magic are the order of the day. When work is going well I know that I'm doing the right thing, but there are days -------! Whether my work betrays any of the aforementioned attributes is for you to decide. I sincerely hope that you enjoy the following pages.

Waiting for the Road

Philip D. Hawkins
Birmingham 1998

Home thoughts

The first three years of my life were spent in a pub, just along the Warwick Road from Tyseley engine sheds in Birmingham. 'The Britannia Inn' was home for me, my parents and grandparents. Just two memories remain of the 'Brit' – the large garden which included a bowling green, and feeding grandad's chickens. He had been a publican for most of his working life and the 'gaffer' of many Birmingham 'boozers'.

In 1950 I moved, with mom and dad of course, across the city to live with great aunt Hetty in Winson Green. The house was a three-up, two-down end of terrace mansion with fading green corporation paintwork (apparently there were two choices, green or brown!). I had reached the grand old age of five when, much to my disgust, a sister arrived. When the midwife came from the bedroom to impart the glad tidings I found a tiny suitcase, packed, left the house and waited at the bus-stop down the road – I had been looking forward to a brother. My freedom was short-lived however and I was promptly marched back into the house, up to my bedroom and introduced to Janet.

Inside the house breathing space was at a premium, but that didn't matter because the centre of my universe was our backyard which, depending on the time of year, was a football stadium or a cricket pitch with stumps carefully chalked on the back door, and a vast road network for my Dinky toy collection. The fact that this wondrous place, with an area of at least ten square yards, was an uneven collection of blue bricks, cunningly laid on a 1 in 2 slope merely added to the drama when Freddie Trueman (dad) bowled to Colin Cowdrey (me) up the slope against the chalk stumps. Five-day tests took up to an hour, unless tea was early, and the outside lavatory door and coal house were witness to a thousand boundaries.

As if all of this excitement wasn't enough, through the back-gate, across the entry (also known as the back passage) and over the railings was the eighth wonder of this small boy's world, the railway embankment – my bank! It was in fact the Soho loop line, a useful operational link from the main New Street to Wolverhampton route at Soho Junction to Perry Barr Junction on the Aston to Wolverhampton line. A former LNWR stronghold, and later LMS, but during the period in question, the London, Midland Region of British Railways held sway.

Across this stage strutted my mechanical heroes. Star turns were the Glasgow train, actually empty stock en route from Duddeston carriage sidings to New Street station, invariably hauled by a Crewe North 'Royal Scot', and 'The Midlander' which was the preserve of Bushbury's stud of well-kept 'Jubilees'. The 'Glasie' came up the bank at 10.50 am and 'The Midlander' down the bank at about 8 pm. There was a steady

The author aged 2½, with friend, on holiday at Cliftonville in 1950.

Right: *As mentioned in the text, cowboys and indians were 'in' in a big way in the 1950s. Inspired no doubt by comics, books and Saturday morning matinees at the local 'fleapit' the Regal. The author is modelling a natty cowboy suit in the front 'garden' at home in 1953, aged 5½.*

One of several school 'mug' shots. This time sporting a 'red indian' tie. Taken at Christmas 1954, aged 7.

A collection of decrepit 'fivers' as mentioned in the text with No. 58169 to the fore in this Sunday scene at Bescot in the late 1950s. The shed's allocation far outstripped its covered accommodation and on Sundays engines would occupy most of the yard area. They would be in light steam in preparation for Mondays workings and this weekly spectacle was known locally as the 'Sunday Roast'. At this time some of these 'fivers' were getting on for 80 years old and looked and sounded every year of it! Designed by Samuel Johnson for the Midland Railway they were built between 1875 and 1902 and originally totalled some 875 engines. (Author's collection)

stream of goods trains which, when climbing the gradient, would usually require the assistance of a banking engine in the shape of an Ivatt Class 2 Mogul from Aston Sheds. Nos 46423 and 46492 spring to mind. Most of these trains were trip workings and often seemed to contain sludge tenders. Favourite freight engines were the ex LNWR 'Super Ds' known to us as 'Duck 8s', Fowler 4Fs were 'Duck 6s', Stanier Class 5s were 'Blackies' and 8Fs were 'Consuls', to mention but a few. A gruesome collection of decrepit ex Midland 2F 0-6-0s, usually from Bescot, also put in regular appearances and were known to one and all as 'Fivers'. Of all the locomotive types to cross 'my bank' my favourites were the 'Patriots'. Though not as glamorous as the 'Scots', their straightforward, no-nonsense demeanour topped off by that odd, pinched-in chimney appealed to me and I always think of them as 'proper' engines.

So much for the LMR line, but just a short distance down the bank these tracks crossed the Western main line from Snow Hill to Wolverhampton, consequently a few yards from my house it was possible to see both lines from a

position between the bridges. During the evenings, weekends and school holidays this spot was a popular rendezvous for local spotters. The Western line was much busier with the regular expresses on the Paddington run producing 'Castles' and 'Kings' in abundance with other passenger services supplying a steady diet of all the 4-6-0 types and Moguls. Local trains were worked by large Prairie tanks and there was plenty of goods traffic too with 2-8-0s, Moguls and the occasional 4700 for good measure.

What more could a small boy wish for? Would the 'railway bug' have bitten so deeply, or even at all, had we not moved to that house by the 'bank'? I've really no idea, but I do know that trainspotting was as popular amongst boys in the 1950s as computer games are today. It was very much a common interest and high on the 'most popular hobbies' list. Many men, now in their forties and fifties will admit, some grudgingly, that they were once trainspotters. Most of them would also have had train sets.

The idea that railways were the 'be all and end all' of my younger years would be quite wrong, rather it was the thread of interest that connected

countless other pastimes that occupy small boys' heads. Cowboys and Indians were 'in', in a big way in the fifties and many budding 'Cisco Kids' had double-belt holsters with matching Colt 45s beneath a ridiculously oversize stetson. Saturday morning matinees at our local 'fleapit', the Regal, were very popular, the results of which manifested itself with swarms of would be 'Zorros' launching themselves off the tops of advertisement hoardings with school macs tied around the neck acting as a cape. Why didn't girls behave like this? We made carts from old pram wheels and a plank and hurtled through the back entries, emerging on to the main road at break-neck speed. Once, to my horror, landing at the feet of a passing policeman, who said nothing, but later the same evening came to the house for a hushed conversation with dad, who duly gave me a clout around the ear. We were chased out of neighbours' back yards (often grandly referred to as gardens) by irate women, with tea-cloths tied around their heads, who would loudly shriek, 'I know your mother', or, 'I know where you lot live'.

All of this excitement took place within sight or sound of the railway. Looking back of course, this is hardly surprising as we wouldn't have wandered far from home, although at the time it seemed like miles. Time after time I would be in trouble for not returning home at the allotted time after post-school 'playing'. Invariably I would be at a mate's house having told his mom,

Boulton Road school football team at the end of the 1957-58 season when we won the league and the cup (the feat was repeated the following season). Mr Cooper, the headmaster, is on the right and Mr Palfreyman on the left. Yours truly is in the front row on the left, aged 10.

'yes, my mom knows where I am, it's OK'. Or we might be sitting by the railway noting down numbers on a scrap of paper, although what we were really doing was hatching devious plots, swapping bubble gum cards, planning the football team, or any number of things, but the railway was the excuse for these misdemeanours.

Highlights of the year were Christmas and summer holidays. I was very lucky with the latter and usually had two; a week or two with mom, dad and my sister, and a fortnight with my grandparents. We didn't have a car and, like most folk in the fifties, we went by train, sending our luggage, in a huge metal trunk, in advance. In 1956, and the following two years, we stayed in a caravan at Blue Anchor Bay in Somerset. The site was bisected by the Taunton to Minehead line, now the preserved West Somerset Railway. Apart from this the only memorable things about these holidays was one year when my sister was launched from the caravan door when a particularly fierce gust of wind caught the door as she was holding the handle. She described a graceful parabola and landed several yards away in a heap of tears. I can still feel the ringing in my ears after receiving a 'smack' from mom for laughing. Also, whilst enjoying a day out with friends in their sit-up-and-beg Ford Popular, it stalled on Porlock Hill and treated us to a hair-raising ride against the traffic flow before eventually finding an escape road. The fact that there were eight of us on board may not have helped!

Grandad liked the Isle of Wight and the Marine Hotel at Ryde welcomed us many times. Sometimes we would travel to Portsmouth by car, a family friend providing the service, and sometimes by train. I have vague memories of seeing Bulleid Pacifics long before underlining

any in my ABC. The first year that I can remember taking any real notice of the railway whilst on holiday was in 1959. We stayed in a chalet at Dawlish Warren in Devon and the entire fortnight was spent deserting the family on the beach and watching trains on the sea-wall. This was the first year that the 'Warship' diesels were in regular service but 90 per cent of trains were still steam hauled. The following year was spent at Exmouth and it was infuriating to see the procession of trains passing through Starcross, in the distance across the River Exe, and being unable to see the numbers. More about holidays later...

My education began in 1952, at Boulton Road Junior and Infants School, ten minutes walk from home. From the main playground, as if by divine intervention, one could see both of the aforementioned railway lines in the middle distance. I was reminded recently that morning 'playtime' coincided with the passage of the Glasgow train and mom would religiously make a note of the engine number. This would be my first question when I eventually came home, although the 'Scot' or sometimes a rebuilt

'Patriot' would most likely have been seen many times before.

I enjoyed my time at Boulton Road, especially the hundred-a-side football matches played with every conceivable type of ball, except a proper football. Many boys served their time being tended by nurse Bonner after being struck in a delicate place with a lethal sorbo rubber ball. Football was as important as trains and dad took me regularly to Villa Park. When the Villa were playing 'away' we would go to the Hawthorns or occasionally Fellows Park. During the last two years at junior school I was a regular member of the football team and Saturdays or Sundays and spring evenings saw us traipsing across our side of the city to play 'away' games. Perry Hall Park was a regular venue, where, as luck would have it, Sunday diversions from the West Coast Main Line passed by in a shallow cutting. Some of these matches would continue well over time because of the mass exodus from the pitch each time a train went by. The sight of a 'Semi' or a 'Princess' was not to be missed!

Meanwhile I found school lessons a bit of a 'doddle', only doing what I had to do, which resulted in reports unanimous in their opinion that 'Philip doesn't try' and 'scatterbrain'. However I always tried when it came to art and was encouraged by one or two teachers and the headmaster Mr Cooper, to produce 'special' pictures for school plays and displays etc. It's a good feeling, when 9 or 10 years old, to be asked to do something 'special', although I don't recall feeling grateful at the time because it sometimes meant missing out on playtime or staying after school. The praise was enjoyable though. Other lessons claimed barely adequate attention, enough to get me by. Nevertheless, when the time came, I passed the 11+ examination and duly went to Lordswood Boys' Technical School in September 1959. This necessitated a short bus ride and very often an aunt would be the conductress and I wouldn't have to pay.

Just before Christmas 1959 I arrived home from school as usual and was surprised to find grandad chatting in an animated way with mom and dad. Now this was really out of the ordinary because grandad was not known for his visits. We would always visit him and did so regularly. I had a terrible feeling that something was wrong. It should be said at this stage that grandad (I only knew one) and I were as thick as thieves. He took me on holiday, bought me great Christmas presents and spoilt me in general. Back to this 'royal' visit. A couple of years previously he had semi-retired as a publican and bought an off-licence and general stores in Acocks Green. Apparently, I discovered later, things were getting on top of him and he was here in an attempt to persuade us to go and live with him so that mom and dad could run the shops. Great, I thought, his new place was much bigger than ours and had a huge garden with a stream running through it. Mom wasn't keen on the idea to say the least, but

a few weeks after Christmas we moved and left behind 'my bank' forever!

Discovering sheds

Throughout my childhood, several members of my family occasionally mentioned in passing, that my great-grandfather Allen had been an engine driver. One would have thought that such a snippet of information given to a railway mad kid would have made him sit up and take notice, but it hardly made any impression at all and I honestly can't remember the subject surfacing again until in my late twenties when mom, who had been sorting through some family 'junk', gave me a faded newspaper cutting from the *Birmingham Evening Mail* celebrating great-grandfather's retirement after a railway career of 50 years. Apparently, he had been an engine driver at Monument Lane sheds in Birmingham when the London & North Western Railway and later the London, Midland & Scottish were in control. He began his career as an engine cleaner at Vauxhall

and soon moved to Monument Lane eventually becoming a driver. According to the newspaper tribute: 'There had been memorable occasions when Royal personages had been entrusted to his care. He has driven troop trains, race trains and in fact every sort of train one could mention!'. There was no date attached to the cutting but I would calculate that his career spanned the years 1880 until 1930.

Perhaps because of this distant family association Monument Lane became the first shed that I actually visited. It was, I believe, in 1958 when dad had the brilliant idea that I would enjoy such a visit. To witness at close quarters from ground level the very same engines that had become old friends on 'my bank' was a magical experience. Suddenly they were seen in an entirely new light with such powerful presence, not to mention the almost human noises that emanated from various parts of their anatomy. Here were the fire-breathing monsters in their lair being tended, fed and watered before venturing forth into the world of mere mortals. My favourite 4F was there, No. 44444, and I was allowed on to the footplate where a patient

A trio of 'Black 5s' at Saltley at 7th March 1965 with No. 45202 on the turntable. After 'bunking' this shed we would often sit beside the line at the back of the yard to savour the action on the New Street to Derby line and the antics of the banking engines on the Camp Hill route. (David K. Morris)

Fifty Years on the Footplate.

One would have thought that the driving of railway trains, including fast-running expresses, would have proved such a nerve-racking experience that, after a much shorter period at the work than 50 years, a man would be approaching a physical and nervous wreck. Not so Mr. R. V. Allen who, having completed the half century of railway work almost wholly spent on the footplate, is retiring from the service of the London, Midland and Scottish Railway at the end of this month. Hale and hearty he has to wear a white beard in order to convince people that he lacks but 13 months the age of seventy.

When Mr. Allen started as an engine cleaner at Vauxhall the famous gardens still flourished. In 1881 he was removed to Monument Lane with a wage of 2s. 6d. a day. But he soon began to climb the ladder. There have been memorable occasions when Royal personages have been entrusted to his care. He has driven troop trains, race trains and in fact every sort of train one could mention.

Mr. Allen has enjoyed remarkably good health throughout his fifty years' service, having been absent from the footplate on two occasions only. He has had one other hobby in addition to his engine, and that has been the very delightful one of gardening.

The newspaper cutting commemorating my great-grandfather's retirement from the footplate. Taken from the Birmingham Evening Mail, *c1930, this was passed to me by my mother who found it while sifting through family 'junk' in the 1970s.*

engineman explained what made it tick. I'm sure that dad had no idea what he had started but after this experience, just watching trains pass by and at stations was no longer quite enough and during the next seven or eight years most engine sheds, or to use the proper terminology, motive power depots, in England, Scotland and Wales were visited, usually unofficially.

By this time, usually in the company of two or three friends, I had begun to spread my wings after the Monument Lane episode had whetted my appetite for more sheds. Maybe, at just 10 or 11 years old we shouldn't have been gallivanting about on trains, on the pretext of 'playing' at a friend's house and mom would surely have gone raving mad, and sometimes did, but the urge was strong.

The first 'far away' shed discovered was Wolverhampton Stafford Road. We soon realised that by catching a train from our local station, Handsworth & Smethwick, to Wolverhampton Low Level and then a local train to the next stop at Dunstall Park, that access to the shed yard was easy to gain from the platform. At once, 'Castles', 'Kings' and 'Halls', most of which had

already been seen at the bottom of my road, were paraded before us and as a bonus the LMR line from the High Level station to Stafford and Crewe ran across the shed yard on a series of bridges. The turntable and coaling stage were some distance from the shed and we would often sit eating sandwiches and swigging Tizer watching the procession of engines being coaled and turned. Stafford Road must have been the tattiest, most filthy shed on the Western. Sometimes the whole of the shed yard was covered in piles of ash and clinker and on windy days this was blended with smoke and steam to create a layer of gritty fog up to chimney level across the entire complex. Today's 'health and safety at work' officials would have it closed down in an instant, as they surely would with many railway installations. Often we would then walk along the canal towpath to Oxley shed which I will always associate with the dreadful smell, especially on hot days, from the pig farm which was adjacent to the pathway leading to the shed yard. This was a busy freight depot and there were usually two or three of the lovely 47XX 2-8-0s which would have escaped our attention at home because they invariably worked during the night.

The local sheds at Tyseley, Saltley and Aston were soon added to the list and little by little the area of operation widened. In 1959 I was lucky enough to travel on a special train to Doncaster Works and shed hauled by Midland Compound No. 1000. Apart from a brief visit to King's Cross station earlier the same year and seeing the odd B1 4-6-0 at New Street, this was the first time that I had been confronted with so many Eastern Region engines and also my first

The second shed visited by the author. Wolverhampton Stafford Road c1960 displays the piles of ash and general debris lying in wait to create the fondly remembered 'foggy grit' when the wind got up. Pannier tank No. 3615 and a double-chimney 'Castle' No. 5073 Blenheim *take centre stage with another 'Castle', No. 4092 Dunraven Castle in the background. (Author's collection)*

A very mixed line-up inside one of Tyseley's roundhouses on 19th September 1965 when the long-familiar 84E shedcode had disappeared to be replaced by 2A under the auspices of the London, Midland Region. No. 6831 Bearley Grange, minus name and numberplates, had earlier worked an excursion into Snow Hill. 'Black 5' No. 44932, an Ivatt Mogul and a Prairie tank complete the scene. (Author)

experience of a locomotive works, the first of many.

Early in 1960, soon after starting my senior school education, I joined the Birmingham Locospotters Club and immediately began travelling the length and breadth of the country, mainly by coach, on Sunday shed-bashing trips. These were interspersed with self-planned outings with friends which often involved a midnight departure from New Street to such places as Leeds, Liverpool, Manchester and Carlisle which gave us the whole of Sunday in which to follow Ian Allan's shed directory to 'bunk' as many depots as possible in these cities, often returning home just in time to grab a few hours sleep before school on Monday. Such outings were far more enjoyable to me than the organised club trips, involving, as they often did, some convoluted train and bus connections in an attempt to complete our planned itinerary which added to the excitement and sense of achievement. However, travelling with the club was excellent value for money and usually cost far less than our own efforts.

It must have been around this time that mom and dad resigned themselves to the fact that their son was rarely at home and stopped including me in family arrangements. Even when trains weren't on the agenda, football was! Dad would occasionally have his Sunday night relaxation interrupted, having been working in the off-licence until 10 pm, by a 'phone call explaining that my money had run out and, was there any chance of a lift? Usually the plea would be made from somewhere fairly local but I remember one rescue mission to Crewe and another to Rugby. Whatever his faults he could always be relied upon in an emergency.

Local sheds were regular haunts, particularly during school-day evenings, when we would regularly cycle to Tyseley, Saltley and Aston, in that order, to see if any foreigners were on shed. Aston was sometimes difficult to 'bunk' and was also home to a homicidal maniac engineman who would take great delight in hurling 'ovoids' of coal which would ricochet along the flanks of rows of engines making a thunderous din as we desperately tried to escape. At Saltley, after checking out the shed, we would sometimes settle down by the neck of the yard and watch

trains on the New Street to Derby line and were occasionally treated to the sight of an Eastern engine which had worked into Birmingham and would retire to Saltley for servicing. These were usually B1s but I remember a couple of V2s and a K1. Heavy freight trains for the Bristol route would also stop near here to take on banking assistance, provided by a Saltley 3F or 4F for the steep climb up to Camp Hill.

One of the most exciting trips was to Scotland in the spring of 1962. During a memorable week I 'finished off' my 'Semis', 'Prinnies' and 'Scots' – Nos 46223 *Princess Alice* and 46121 *Highland Light Infantry, City of Glasgow Regiment* at Polmadie (66A) and 46201 *Princess Elizabeth* at Carlisle Kingmoor (12A). Quite an army of ex Caledonian veterans were still intact with many still working but the highlight was seeing the 'rare' 'Jubilees' at Corkerhill (67A) and to a lesser extent at Kingmoor. Most 'Brummie' spotters had similar gaps in their 'Jubilee' collection and to see the likes of *Neptune, Agamemnon, Lord Rutherford of Nelson, Valiant, Keppel,* and many more was an ambition fulfilled. Sadly, some were in store never to turn a wheel again, but I only became aware of this later.

Trains Illustrated magazine was discovered in 1960 and the monthly ritual of entering reallocations and withdrawals into my shed 'ref' provided up to date information of where everything was and added a further element to planning trips.

Locomotive works were something else again. Here it was possible to see engines, sometimes old favourites, being cut up while others would be immaculate, fresh from the paint shop. On occasions, these two extremes would involve

Almost the end of steam at Old Oak Common, on 17th January 1965, with a handful of pannier tanks still hanging on to their empty stock duties into and out of Paddington. A Brush Type 4, later Class 47, defiantly represents the new order. The classic trappings of a steam shed make a fascinating frame as a father and son 'mooch' around. (Author)

engines of the same class. Ex LNWR 'Super Ds' at Crewe and 'Castles' at Swindon for example, and there were many more. I managed to successfully negotiate the works at Crewe, Swindon, Doncaster and Eastleigh without a permit, usually by tagging on to an organised party and making myself invisible, although on one occasion at Swindon I did manage to talk my way in and had a private tour complete with guide. An oft-cited problem of works visits was trying to figure out which dismembered parts of an engine constituted a 'cop'. I seem to remember that we had to see the cabside number and the corresponding smokebox before it counted and that Western Region engines had their number stamped on the coupling rods, over each axle.

Travelling became a way of life and I loved it. Initially the object of the exercise was to 'cop' as many new engine numbers as possible with the

ultimate aim to see them all, but in retrospect there was so much more to it than that. Over a few short years I become acquainted with many of the less fashionable districts of our big cities. Near the entrance to the large freight shed at Speke Junction, about eight miles out of Liverpool, there was a corner shop with a metal grille protecting the window. 'What sort of people live around here?' I wondered in my innocence. It was a fact that most city engine sheds were situated in the less glamorous districts. More affluent areas would never have tolerated the dirt and noise. Or was it that they were able to move elsewhere when the railway moved in? A combination of both I suspect, but it did provide a partial insight into how things

A typical scene inside Saltley shed on 7th March 1965 with 9F No. 92138 receiving attention alongside 'Black 5' No. 44776. The authorities here seemed to tolerate the ever-present nuisance of train-spotters more than most sheds which was surprising considering how busy it was at most times of the day. (David K. Morris)

really were and extended my education beyond the classroom. I became quite adept at finding my way around London's Underground system and bus routes in an attempt to visit all of the Capital's engine sheds in one day. Football excursions were an inexpensive way to travel and we would even see the match if it promised to be good. We were fortunate in Birmingham in that in the early sixties all of the local teams, Aston Villa, West Bromwich Albion and Birmingham City, as well as Wolverhampton Wanderers, were in the 1st or 2nd divisions and provided away matches at regular intervals at Liverpool, Manchester, Sheffield and Leeds giving us a good choice of cheap rail travel throughout the season.

These trainspotting pilgrimages continued with a vengeance until about 1964 when my enthusiasm, for a variety of reasons, waned. One of these was the very obvious rundown of steam power which resulted in such unedifying sights as the remaining Western 4-6-0s running around minus their nameplates leaving three ugly brackets protruding from the splasher. Dirty locomotives were one thing but this was too much and just one of the many manifestations of the almost total lack of care shown by British Railways towards the objects of my affection. One of the rapidly decreasing bright spots was on the Southern Region where Bulleid Pacifics in decent 'nick', were still on top link work out of Waterloo on the ex LSWR main line. Basingstoke became a favourite haunt along with other points west to Weymouth. Even these trips became less frequent as other teenage interests took precedence.

From the age of 10 until 16, thousands of miles were covered, mainly by train, from the north of Scotland to Cornwall. Dozens of notebooks were filled with the spoils of these adventures and I still have most of them from 1961 onwards. Occasionally they will provide inspiration for a painting or solve a problem of reference, but the most important aspect was the experience of travelling and of trudging round engine sheds, often in foul weather ankle deep in ash and oil, breathing in the unmistakable aroma of the steam railway. There was always

something special to see, to discuss and argue about. A regular travelling companion was a school friend, Dave Morris, who could always be relied upon to provide moments of light relief. Hardly a shed visit went by without him disappearing into an inspection pit, walking into point levers or treading in an oil puddle unaware that it was concealing an uncovered man-hole. Many are the times that I turned to chat only to find him gone. A few seconds later a groan, a moan, some choice language and an oil-covered hand slowly rising, excalibur-like, from the pit would confirm that he had done it again. I still see Dave from time to time and remind him of his shed-stuntman days. He denies that it happened with anything like the regularity that I recall – but I'm not so sure.

Maybe British Railways missed out on a substantial source of revenue during the fifties and sixties by not cashing in on the insatiable desire of enthusiasts to go 'shedbashing'. Imagine it – the larger sheds could have set up box offices, open on Sundays only perhaps, with uniformed guides, catalogues, roster lists, footplate rides, photographs, demonstration boiler wash-outs, turntable demonstrations, details of engines away at works or out on loan, the list could go on and on. What a day out that would have been, and infinitely preferable to some of the dubious offerings at today's adventure parks. Perhaps if steam and enthusiasts had lasted into the ultra cost-conscious nineties there would be hoards of anoraks festooned with camera gear queuing outside Crewe North, Old Oak Common, Carlisle Kingmoor, Doncaster, etc, etc

A page from the author's notebook in August 1962 when full use was made of a Cornish railrover ticket with several trips along the Cornish main line to Plymouth. This was the last year of steam in Cornwall and 'Warships' were to the fore. Nevertheless there was a mouth-watering selection of 'Castles', 'Counties' and 'Granges' with a sprinkling of Prairie tanks for good measure. (Author)

on Sunday mornings. Perish the thought! Surely part of the 'buzz' of furtively tip-toeing between rows of engines was the certain knowledge that we shouldn't have been there.

Holidays and trains

As the fifties progressed so it slowly but surely dawned that many of the locomotives that paraded through my local hunting ground were seen again and again. Such things as shedplates and depot allocations entered the equation. Until the spring of 1959 I had to make do with copies of the single volume Ian Allan ABCs, those for the Western and London, Midland regions. The cost of a combined volume at 10s 6d was way out of my reach. Consequently the mysteries of the Southern and Eastern regions gradually unravelled after looking through the combined volumes of more affluent friends. What on earth were these pages full of numbers beginning with '3' and '6'?

It was my good fortune that summer holidays came my way twice a year. Why little notice was taken of these distant railways is a mystery to me now. Perhaps there was just so much else to occupy my time. A fortnight at Dawlish Warren, Devon in 1959 proved to be the breakthrough when hitherto unseen 'Castles', 'Halls,' and many others were added to my collection. It was also the first time that I had been armed with a combined volume 'ref', bought a couple of months earlier at Snow Hill station and taken home with reverence. I couldn't wait to underline Southern and Eastern numbers.

The holiday definitely started well. Tickets were bought well in advance for an excursion train to Devon that departed from Birmingham Moor Street at around midnight on Friday. My memory of the journey is remarkably clear, starting with me wandering off to the front of the train to get the number of 'our' 'Castle', and incurring much parental wrath in the process. It turned out to be No. 4037 *The South Wales Borderers*, a Newton Abbot engine at the time I have since discovered. The entire journey to Bristol was spent hanging from the carriage window amongst luggage piled high along the length of the corridor, in a vain attempt to see anything that passed by. On arrival at Temple Meads some time was spent waiting in the station and a brisk balancing act to the front of the train produced the spectacle of Bath Road sheds illuminated beneath the yard lights. Amongst the expected 'Castles' and 'Halls' were two 'Britannias', one of them, I remember, was No. 70029 *Shooting Star*. That would impress my mates! After what seemed an eternity we reached Exeter in the early hours of Saturday morning and had to change trains for a local to Dawlish Warren. Disembarking at St Davids I could hardly believe my eyes. There, amidst the confusion of passengers, station staff and luggage trolleys, lurking in the shadows, was the unmistakable outline of a Southern 'Pacific'. Once again, for the umpteenth time since leaving Birmingham mom and dad were left to worry as I set off on my quest for a number beginning with '3'. It turned out to be 'Battle of Britain'

No. 34079 *141 Squadron* and it looked magnificent to this 11 year old. Another vivid memory of the next few minutes is of straining my eyes through the side of the footbridge as a 'Warship' enveloped the entire station with vibration and noise as it roared past on the down through road.

Eventually we caught the connection and were deposited at Dawlish Warren. The ensuing two weeks were spent watching trains on the sea-wall and persuading mom and dad to take me to Exeter so that I could spend some time at Central station. How many times it worked I can't remember, but it was several. Sitting on the platforms watching Pacifics, Moguls, T9s, Z class tanks and many more was far better than a matinee at the Regal! *Cunard White Star* was the first 'Merchant Navy' I saw and can remember running my fingers along the huge, gun-metal nameplate, perhaps to make sure that I was really there.

Back on the sea-wall all of the earlier D600 'Warships' were underlined as were most of the D800 series up to No. D809 *Champion*. Several 'Counties' were added to my list and I was surprised, and delighted to see one or two Southern light Pacifics working on the Western. Subsequently this mystery was solved when it was discovered that this was regular practice to allow SR drivers to learn the route to Plymouth just as Western crews did on the SR route.

What a great holiday, and an important summer in other ways because I had left junior school and would start at Lordswood Boys in September. At least I would be armed with some impressive Southern 'cops'.

The following year, 1960, could have been a bit of a let-down holiday-wise because we headed for a fortnight at Exmouth, just across the River Exe from the previous year but too far away to see engine numbers on the sea-wall. To counteract this nondescript railway resort I had taken the precaution of writing to British Railways to apply for permits to visit Laira and Exmouth Junction sheds, in dad's name of course. What the 'powers that be' thought of his handwriting I don't know, but amazingly the

required permits duly arrived just prior to our holiday. They were for a particular date and time and for twelve persons! Recollection of the train journey from Birmingham escapes me except the trip from Exeter Central to Exmouth behind a Standard Class 3 tank. An experience repeated several times during the ensuing two weeks.

We never did make it to Exmouth Junction shed; dad couldn't find it, so he said! Laira, however, was different. Dad and I set out from Exmouth arriving at Exeter Central very early where we caught a train to St Davids. The prospect of a journey along the coast road through Newton Abbot to Plymouth was mouth-watering and the promise of a perfect day began when No. 1024 *County of Pembroke* slid into St Davids with our train. Approaching Plymouth, after running alongside the River Plym, Laira shed yard was in full view and packed with engines. I recall a very smug feeling knowing that shortly we would be paying an official visit. At North Road station we found out which bus to catch for the long ride back out to Laira. On arrival in the shed foreman's office dad did some nifty talking to explain the missing ten persons in our party and eventually an elderly railwayman arrived who was appointed to be our guide. Sadly my notebook no longer exists but I remember several 'Castles', 'Counties', 'Halls' and 'Granges' not seen before and a myriad of tank engines including the tiny saddle tank, No. 1363. Having exhausted every nook and cranny we reported back to the foreman who kindly stamped my 'ref' with the official Laira rubber stamp. He also suggested that we might pay a visit to Friary shed, which we duly did before returning to North Road where, as if to order, 'West Country' No. 34104 *Bere Alston* was waiting to take us back to Exeter.

1961 was a bad year. We went to Folkestone and, apart from one day when I managed to escape on my own to Ashford sheds, a trickle of Southern electrics was the only fare. Later that year dad passed his driving test and at last we had a car. During the war he had been a driver and found himself behind the wheel of anything from Jeeps and staff cars to tank transporters and I could never understand why he had to take a driving test. Be that as it may, he was now the proud owner of a brand new Austin A40 in Sutherland green, an odd looking vehicle, a cross between a saloon and an estate. The bilious colour didn't help either! At the time of writing a near neighbour has one, now a collector's item, and I occasionally gaze inside and wonder how four of us, complete with tons of luggage, managed on our journey to Cornwall in the summer of 1962. This holiday began with a near disaster while searching for our hotel on the outskirts of Newquay. Coming off a steep uphill junction on to a main road our trusty A40 started to tip backwards, too much luggage in the back perhaps! As the bonnet began to rise dad and I, sitting in the front seats, bounced madly up and down in an effort to reach terra-firma. We slid slowly backwards and watched, with great relief, as the bonnet resumed its accustomed position. A unanimous decision was made to avoid that particular junction during the next fortnight.

This was to be the last holiday that we spent together as a family. In subsequent years either mom or dad had to stay behind to look after the shops which were becoming busier. In retrospect I'm very grateful that I took full advantage of the opportunity and bought a rover ticket that allowed unlimited travel in Cornwall. All the main sheds were visited with a trip to Wadebridge, to see the last of the Beattie well tanks, thrown in for good measure. Thankfully I still have the relevant notebook and can confirm that Laira was 'bunked' three times during the fortnight. Other sheds receiving the same treatment were Penzance, St Blazey, Plymouth Friary, Wadebridge and Newton Abbot, although the latter wasn't included in my rover ticket. For some reason Truro was missed, perhaps I was thrown out. 'Warships' were in charge of practically all the top link passenger services in Cornwall by this time with the mediocre, drab looking D6300s on secondary duties although I did see a few 'Counties' and 'Granges' filling in and several steam/diesel combinations. In later years I learnt that 1962

was the official end of steam in the county and, indeed, Penzance lost its allocation at the end of the summer timetable. The first 'Western' class diesels had recently entered traffic and a few were seen at Plymouth where, as a matter of coincidence Nos D1004 *Western Crusader* and 1004 *County of Somerset* were seen together at North Road station. One of the highlights of my wanderings was to ride across the Royal Albert bridge several times, an ambition since Cuneo's marvellous poster featuring Brunel's masterpiece had demanded my attention on many station platforms during the previous year or two.

Unfortunately the box Brownie had remained with the family on the beach at Newquay, and as a result, I have absolutely no photographic record of this most enjoyable fortnight. The notes are some compensation though, parts of which are reproduced here. This was to be my last holiday where trains took priority and 1965 found me staying with three buddies, in a holiday camp at Douglas on the Isle of Man – freedom had arrived along with the mixed delights of wine, women and song. Railways only occasionally claimed my full attention.

The reader may be questioning the relevance of holidays to my present work, with some justification perhaps. In mitigation I would have to say that these recollections, and many others that serve to fuel my imagination, are priceless, as is the very fact of 'being there', the thrill of seeing a rare engine, of walking around Laira sheds surrounded on all sides by the smells and sounds of everyday working steam, the kindness of the foreman, but most of all the excitement and anticipation of setting out on these adventures. Perhaps my enthusiasm could have been directed more usefully elsewhere to other interests but it was the railway that fired my imagination and I was eager to drink in all I possibly could. Now, when confronted with a blank canvas I can draw on these experiences, savour the aroma and hear the sounds. Maybe its the difference between an adequate railway painting and a convincing one. Who knows, but I'm sure of one thing – I wouldn't have missed it for the world!

Palaces of delight – New Street and Snow Hill

During the last 15 years or so New Street and Snow Hill stations have figured in at least a dozen of my paintings of which more than half have been commissioned. City railway stations such as these became an intrinsic part of people's lives, particularly until the late fifties when almost everyone used them at least once a year for their summer holidays and many thousands used them daily as commuters. My father, for example, used the train regularly when we lived in Winson Green to travel to his job as a coach-trimmer at the James motorcycle company in Small Heath, catching the Prairie-hauled local at Soho & Winson Green and travelling across the city through Snow Hill. Such stations were considered with deep affection by countless citizens, others of course could take them or leave them, but not many I think. the deep emotions felt for Snow Hill surfaced in the late sixties with the unbelievable announcement from British Railways that it was to close. How could such a once-crucial part of the city disappear? Anyone who knew about such things was aware that New Street could barely function smoothly at the best of times, let alone with the extra traffic generated by the closure of its once-great rival.

The death of Snow Hill was slow and undignified, main line services ceased in 1967 and local trains gradually disappeared until the last one, a single unit railcar operating all stations to Wolverhampton, ran for the last time in 1972. The full realisation of the station's impending demise finally dawned for many Brummies late in 1969 and early 1970 when the once-impressive façade and Great Western hotel were reduced to rubble and the gap between the platforms was filled in to form a car park. The unthinkable had happened and the folly of closure was realised too late to save the old station.

A new Snow Hill was built and opened to passengers in 1988 on the same site with none of the former grandeur, but at least trains are running through the tunnel again.

Although taken as late as 24th July 1965 this picture epitomises the quieter moments at Snow Hill with a pannier tank, No. 9608, trundling a trip freight along the up through line passing a couple of pigeons. The view also gives a good impression of the light and airy atmosphere of this much-loved and lamented station. (David K. Morris)

New Street didn't quite reach the hearts of Brummies in the same way as Snow Hill, perhaps because it was bigger, busier, dirtier, more confusing and not as attractive, but in a way it was much more a part of the city. A public way, Queens Drive, divided the North Western and Midland platforms and busy city roads surrounded the entire station. Complete rebuilding, begun in 1964 and completed in 1967, almost obliterated the station that I knew as a kid and created an underground concrete tomb with a corresponding character. At the time of writing there is talk of building a new inter-city station for Birmingham in the newly

designated district of Heartlands just outside the city centre. This would leave New Street to cater for local traffic only.

Train mad kids in Birmingham were fortunate in that both stations presented examples of almost every locomotive type from the London, Midland and Western regions. The only notable types missing were 'Duchesses' and 'Princesses' and even these could be seen on Sundays when West Coast traffic was diverted, and although New Street was by-passed, a short train ride to Aston or Stechford was all that was required to see them. Also, when diesels took over many West Coast Pacific duties in the early sixties 'Duchesses' were then sometimes used on Wolverhampton to Euston trains which ran through New Street.

When exactly I first discovered these two palaces of delight in the centre of Birmingham is lost in the mists of time but it almost certainly

It is late in 1962 and the 'Western' diesel-hydraulics have recently ousted the mighty 'Kings' on Paddington expresses. No. D1001 Western Pathfinder, *resplendent in maroon livery, stands bathed in sunlight at Platform 7 in charge of a Paddington train. I was always fond of these engines and photographed them extensively in the early 1970s. (Author's Collection)*

involved family holidays. Snow Hill was the first I came to know well. Our school football team would often meet for away matches outside the main entrance and to kill time, waiting for late-comers, we would wander around the grand concourse, with boots dangling around our necks, peering into the large glass display cases that contained the wares of local companies. It wasn't long after this that entire days were spent on the platforms. My lasting impression of Snow Hill is of a very well ordered, light and airy station. A vantage point at either end would allow everything to be seen with the added attraction at the up end of the spectacle of trains erupting from the long tunnel from Moor Street. During quieter periods there was plenty to occupy our inquisitive minds, including putting pennies into a bright red machine which would stamp out our names, and other less choice phrases, on a metal strip. One of the bay platforms at the north end was the scene of my first footplate ride, together with a couple of mates. It may have been just a few yards but the illicit journey aboard Prairie tank No. 4175 made us feel like we'd won the pools!

There was a steady flow of Paddington expresses which included the 'Inter-City' and the 'Cambrian Coast Express', almost exclusively hauled by 'Kings' and 'Castles' with 'Halls', 'Granges' and the odd 'Manor' and Mogul on secondary services. The 'Cornishman' made up a trio of named trains seen here. Prairie tanks fussed in and out with local trains until about 1958 when DMUs began to take over. A Great Western railcar regularly worked the 'Dudley dodger'. The through tracks were often occupied by freight trains waiting for the road and pannier tanks scurried through with great regularity. 'Counties' were the most scarce passenger types and were usually greeted with shrieks of delight by the waiting rabble. On the other hand, many 'Castles' and 'Kings' were seen so often that they were booed and slandered as 'crates'. The 'King' with the bell, No. 6000 *King George V*, better known to us as 'King Ding', was subject to this humiliation countless times.

There is no doubt that Snow Hill was a fine station but as soon as I got to know New Street, in all its polluted glory, there was no contest for my affections, what a place this was and the exact opposite of Snow Hill. It was much noisier, dirtier, busier, far more chaotic and, to this kid at least, it had atmosphere, loads and loads of atmosphere. To me it was everything a large station should be and I found the locomotives more interesting too. It seemed that the only local main line engines seen there were the Bushbury 'Jubes', everything else came from – well, everywhere. Crewe North, Camden, Holbeck, Derby, Trafford Park, Bristol Barrow Road and many more depots contributed to the never-ending variety to delight youthful connoisseurs of motive power at New Street.

The layout of the station, with its two distinct sections, made it necessary to choose a vantage point carefully so as not to miss anything – heaven forbid. My favourite pitch was at the east end of Platform 6 adjacent to signalbox No. 1 where, in a siding, were usually one or two open wagons loaded with the station's refuse. The smell from this, particularly on a hot summer day, was powerful and combined with the ever present scent of fish permeating through from the Midland side made a potent cocktail. Smoke and steam paled into insignificance by comparison. 'Scots', 'Jubes' and 'Black 5s' could always be seen in the North Western platforms and the latter two types were also common over on the Midland where Bristol's three 'Patriots', Nos 45504, 45506 and 45519, were also regulars, the latter, *Lady Godiva* becoming a firm favourite. Standard designs were represented by regular visits from Class 4 and Class 5 4-6-0s and, to a lesser extent, 'Britannias'. As with the GWR Prairie tanks over at Snow Hill, Stanier 2-6-2 and 2-6-4 tanks and Fowler 2-6-4Ts did the fussing at New Street. The period in question here is 1958 until 1963, and I can just remember 2P 4-4-0s and Compounds but they had almost gone in my heyday apart from Nos 40936 and 41168 which lingered on in store at Monument Lane sheds until late in 1961.

Unlike Snow Hill, New Street was an 'open'

station and as such you didn't require a platform ticket to set foot into the grandstand. This had the added advantage to us kids in that we could come and go as we pleased, particularly useful when told to scram by station staff, only to reappear a few minutes later as if nothing had happened. There was rarely a dull moment at New Street, even if only passing by on the top deck of a bus. When I had to travel to school from Acocks Green to Bearwood I would sometimes travel via the city centre and well remember 'copping' a Holbeck 'Scot', No. 46109 *Royal Engineer*, one morning in 1960.

Named trains using the station were the 'Pines Express', the 'Devonian' and the 'Midlander'. The latter has been mentioned before in these pages and will be familiar to readers by now. The 'Devonian' was invariably worked by one of Bristol Barrow Road's 'Jubes', not always in the best of condition, externally at least. As with 'King Ding' over at Snow Hill, the likes of *Shovell*, *Trafalgar*, *Leander*, *Kempenfelt*, *Barfleur*, *Rooke* and *Galatea*, were loudly booed by the gallery during their frequent visits. Derby 'Jubes' were also used on this train ensuring visits from *Seychelles*, *Wemyss*, *Basutoland* and others. Oddly enough, I only remember seeing my namesake, No. 45649, in New Street a handful of times even though it was a Derby engine.

The panorama from the east end of Platform 6 provided a good view of arrivals and departures from both the North Western and Midland sides and also offered a superb broadside angle of Euston departures and so forth from Platform 3. Memories of 'Scots' waiting for take-off come flooding back, occasionally they would have been double-headed with a 'Black 5' or 'Jube'. I distinctly remember Nos 45709 *Implacable* and 46153 *The Royal Dragoon* in this very situation sometime in 1961, and actually took a photograph with my plastic camera. Unfortunately there was only room for the 'Scot', and just the tender of the 'Jube'. I swear that there was plenty of scope in the viewfinder for the complete engine.

During the fifties main line diesels in the shape

Double-headed trains were a common sight at New Street. Here, a Standard Class 5, No. 73141, and 'Jubilee' No. 45626 Seychelles stand at Platform 9 at the head of a Bristol train. This is the old Midland Railway side with signalbox No. 4 on the right and box No. 5 visible in the background through the bridge. (Author's collection)

of the ex LMS Co-Cos Nos 10000 and 10001 and the ex Southern trio, Nos 10201–10203 had become familiar to me, but the year 1958 saw other more portentous main line arrivals in the form of Sulzer Bo-Bos of the D5000 series, later to become Class 24s. Early examples could be seen in New Street, often with trains to Rugby and Peterborough, and were thought of as a brief aberration. How could these puny looking machines compete with Staniers 4-6-0s? Little did we know, in our youthful innocence, that this

was the beginning of the end, and by 1960, some of the Bristol line trains were in the hands of the more impressive looking 'Peaks' while English Electric Type 4s, later known as Class 40s, were seen regularly on North Western line trains. During the following two or three years these two types had practically ousted steam from passenger services. At Snow Hill similar changes were happening and by the end of 1962, 'Western' class diesels had sent the mighty 'Kings' to their doom. It all happened so quickly

and yet I don't recall recognising the signs until it was too late.

Maybe I have given the impression that my preference was for New Street and that would be correct, although if a time-travel ticket came my way with the proviso that only Snow Hill was on the agenda, then I would go back like a shot. I'm glad that both of them become so familiar to me, but for sheer spectacle and atmosphere New Street won hands down.

Earlier I mentioned that the only main line

A view from the author's favourite vantage point at New Street, the eastern end of Platform 6, with a brace of local trains preparing to leave, watched by a small gallery of young 'Brummies'. A Fowler 2-6-4 tank, No. 42320, is at Platform 3 and Stanier 2-6-2 tank No. 40125 at Platform 4. This is the old London & North Western side where the overall roof was removed after the war following bomb damage. (Author's collection)

passenger engines not to frequent New Street were 'Duchesses' and 'Princesses'. Since becoming the proud owner of a Hornby-Dublo *Duchess of Montrose* when the model was first introduced in 1953, I longed to see those magnificent machines in the flesh. My wish came true during the course of a school day trip by train to Southport in 1958. As our special train passed slowly through Crewe station there it

was, probably ex-works and shining like a new pin – No. 46232 *Duchess of Montrose*. 'Sir, sir, I've got that one!', I yelled. Whether or not 'sir' knew about trains, I've no idea, but I recall that he showed some interest before telling me to calm down and to stop hanging out of the window before I got my head knocked off! The sight of 'my' 'Duchess' made me determined to see more and by 1959 we were 'clued up' enough

about their workings to plan a summer Saturday trip to the West Coast Main Line. My companions were a couple of school friends. We made our way to New Street, caught a DMU to Lichfield City and walked to Trent Valley station. We were impatient and the walk seemed to take forever. I've since discovered that the distance is just over one mile. On arrival we spied the main gallery, just off the south end of

The southbound 'Devonian' running into Platform 10 behind Bristol 'Jubilee' No. 45651 Shovell. This particular engine seemed to be in and out of New Street several times a day and must surely have carried the most unglamorous but appropriate name ever given to a steam locomotive. In the background, an ex Midland 0-6-0, No. 43687, rests against signalbox No. 2 between station pilot duties while just visible behind its tender is the fence at the end of Platform 6 upon which the author and countless other kids perched to witness the New Street comings and goings. (Author's collection)

the platforms on the down side, and rushed to join the madding throng. Just then a red blur hurtled by at terrific speed. I realised that it was a 'Princess', but couldn't make out the number. We joined the rabble and discovered that it was No. 46207 *Princess Arthur of Connaught* (strange name for a princess), my first 'Prinnie'. What a great day it turned out to be, we saw

about 15 'Semies', another three or four 'Prinnies' and lots of 'Jubes', 'Scots' and 'Patriots'. Many of these appeared later in the day on return workings.

We soon learnt to identify the numbers even though the average speed must have been 80 to 90 mph. The terms 'peg on the clanger' and 'peg on the main' became part of our vocabulary and

could also be used at Tamworth, a location explored shortly after this trip. Here, the New Street to Derby main line crossed the West Coast tracks and produced 'Jubes' and 'Black 5s' in abundance on a summer Saturday. Mean-hearted firemen of southbound engines on the Midland line would sometimes infuriate us by dangling their cotton-waste rag over the last digits of the cabside number making it impossible to read. If it was a 'namer' and clean then this was no problem but otherwise we just hoped that someone on the high level platforms had the answer.

Nuneaton and Rugby soon entered the West Coast equation. Rugby in particular was a marvellous location, in addition to the Great Central line crossing over our heads on the famous bird-cage bridge, there was the engine shed and the test plant. Double-headed 9Fs rattling loudly across the bridge on the 'Windcutter' freights remain a vivid memory as does my first sight of a North Eastern B16. Engines would constantly potter along to the turntable close to the bridge and liven up the few quieter moments, and there was always the sheds to 'bunk'.

The reader must bear in mind that these are memories from over 30 years ago, and we all know that some things improve with age. A year to a child seems like a lifetime, hours and hours spent watching trains at Birmingham's premier stations and loitering with intent by the West Coast Main Line seemed the most natural way to

spend our time. Judging by the armies of balaclava-clad kids seen on Saturdays noisily occupying platform ends and grassy banks, it was a common conclusion. Hopefully these brief recollections will give some idea of what inspires my work. Photographs, of course, are invaluable images to refresh our memories and without the efforts of those who were willing, able and aware enough to record those exciting days on film for posterity, where would artists such as myself be? – but the most important element from my point of view are the personal memories. Elusive elements such as sounds, smells and the feeling of anticipation and excitement rarely emerge from a photograph and these ephemeral qualities are what I attempt to portray through my paintings.

Muck, grime and decline

It is often said that nostalgia is dishonest and judging by many artistic offerings depicting days gone by, when every Christmas was white and June was always flaming, then perhaps this statement is correct. Railway art is probably

more susceptible than most to perpetuating this myth. As an artist I am occasionally torn between a client's rose-tinted recollections and my own preference for 'telling it like it was', to coin a phrase, or at least how I think it was.

Anyone of my vintage or older who has any knowledge at all of railways whether as a railwayman, passenger, enthusiast or even someone who happened to live by or near the railway will know from experience that steam railways were inherently filthy, very filthy indeed. Remember finding a seat in a compartment carriage, sitting down and disappearing in a cloud of smoky dust from the jazzy patterned, moquette-covered seat or experiencing a sauna bath in winter when the steam heating leaked beneath the seat enshrouding everything in sight with steam? Wearing your best gear was not recommended when travelling by train in the days of steam.

Maintaining locomotives, rolling stock, stations, engine sheds and other installations in anything like a presentable condition required far more attention and resources than British Railways could muster. Consequently, from the beginning of the Second World War, through the fifties until the end of steam in 1968, a clean engine was, more often than not, an indication that it was recently out of the paint shop rather than being well cared for. Low wages on the railway were not conducive to attracting workers who could find better paid jobs with more pleasant working conditions in most other industries. After the war until the sixties there was virtually full employment in Great Britain and workers could afford to be choosy to a certain extent. Certainly, motive power depots in the larger cities and towns found it practically impossible to recruit cleaning staff. Even so, passenger locomotives, particularly from the top

Worcester shed enjoyed a reputation for keeping its 'Castles' clean, exemplified here by No. 5083 Bath Abbey *seen backing out of Paddington after bringing in an express in the mid 1950s. (Author's collection)*

This picture illustrates the difficulty that we had deciphering the cast numberplates on grubby Western engines. Although a fairly close-up view of a Churchward 2-8-0 in typical condition, trundling through Gloucester Central in the early '50s, its number, 2835, is barely readable. (Author's collection)

links, were generally turned out in a presentable condition, indeed several depots earned quite a reputation, against all odds, for the immaculate turn-out of their star inmates.

Bushbury 'Jubilees' for example, most of which I saw day after day during the fifties, were invariably 'spick and span' and carried some most evocative names into the bargain. *Meteor, Samson, Atlas,* and *Polyphemus,* spring readily to mind and were to me amongst man's most glamorous creations. When they proudly carried the 'Midlander' headboard the vision seemed complete. Worcester shed too could always be relied upon to look after its 'Castles' for the Paddington expresses. Similar examples of pride in the job could be found at other sheds throughout the country, often through the ceaseless efforts of individual shed-masters, but they were swimming against the tide.

Hindsight is an alarmingly precise science and we now realise that Britain's steam railway was rapidly entering its death throes. Kids of the period simply saw what they saw and there was little to indicate that the end of a glorious era was but a few years away. After all, brand new Standard locomotives were still being built and this was confirmed by our Ian Allan ABCs by the reassuring phrase beneath whole classes, 'Engines of this class are still being delivered'. We knew that steam engines had a long shelf life, an average of at least 30 years, so what could possibly happen to annihilate them before say – 1990? The rest, as they say, is history!

Little had changed since the turn of the century, steam reigned supreme, semaphore signals guarded the tracks, there were thousands of signalboxes, hundreds of engine sheds and the ambition of many small boys was still to be

This 'Grange', No. 6848 Toddington Grange, is unusual in that it retains its name and numberplates at this late stage of Western steam, although its condition is typical. A scene at Old Oak Common on 17th January 1965. (Author)

engine drivers, so perhaps we could be forgiven for thinking that things would be all right for the next 20 or 30 years at least. Small clues to the contrary came our way. Occasionally a brand new Sulzer Type 3 diesel (later Class 33) would shyly emerge from the nearby Birmingham Railway Carriage & Wagon works and scuttle past en route for duty on the Southern Region. Grandad presented me with a Hornby-Dublo Bo-Bo diesel, No. D8000 by request, for Christmas 1958, or was it '59? 'You've waited for it, and its worth it' ran the blurb in *Meccano Magazine* – how could I resist? Diesel multiple units were taking over local services from Prairie tanks on the Western and during my 1959 holiday in Devon, 'Warship' diesels were wearing 'Torbay Express' and 'Cornish Riviera Express' headboards, once the property of 'Castles' and 'Kings'.

Maybe the one event that made me wonder about the future of steam was when the 'Westerns' craftily usurped the 'Kings' on Paddington expresses during the second half of 1962. At this time I would often sit on my bike on Tyseley bridge during the evenings watching trains. One by one the 'Kings' disappeared and the 'Westerns', some green, some maroon and one in that strange 'desert sand' livery, slowly but surely muscled their way in. My notebooks reveal that a visit to Stafford Road sheds in September confirmed my fears – there, lying cold and dead, some with sacks over the chimney, were no less than nine 'Kings'. Old friends snatched away without a word.

I digress, back to muck and grime. Collecting numbers was often infuriating where really dirty engines were concerned, particularly on the Western lines. Many panniers, Moguls and 2-8-0s passed by without fear of being identified. The small, cast number plates were so well camouflaged by layers of dirt that some escaped our notebooks. Often, one of our number would be posted actually on the embankment close to the line in an effort to decipher the front number plate. Fortunately the freight trains hauled by these engines were not famous for their speed exploits and between us there was usually

enough time to figure out if the engine was a 'cop' or not. 'Kings' and 'Castles' on this line were a mixed bunch when it came to cleanliness but I seem to remember that many appeared to be in good nick. It's a strange thing but to this kid engines on the Western always gave the impression of being smaller and fussier, with their copper-capped chimneys and brass adornments, than the Midland 'Scots' and 'Jubes' for example. Even 9Fs and WDs looked smaller when seen on the Western!

Many readers will consider the following remark as sacrilege – but I soon tired of the 'Kings' as I had seen them all by about 1956 with the exception of No. 6014 *King Henry VII*, a Stafford Road engine, which somehow escaped my attention until 1959. How this happened I've no idea, but according to my notes it did! 'Castles', on the other hand, were always welcomed, especially those with the aircraft names which seemed particularly glamorous with that little bit extra beneath the nameplate which read 'Castle Class'. Why didn't the 'Earls' have this?

'Halls', 'Granges' and 'Manors' were often as filthy as the purely freight engines and were sometimes difficult to identify which was annoying because we knew that many came from far-flung sheds and would surely have been 'cops'. My favourites on the Western were the 'Counties', due partly no doubt to their rarity value but also because they looked so different to the company's other passenger engines with their straight nameplates and hunched-up appearance when fitted with double chimneys. Also it was difficult to see the entire class with many allocated to Cornish and Welsh sheds. Perhaps this added to their special aura.

Back on the Midland line 'Scots' that appeared on the Glasgow train always seemed to be clean with many also having the added embellishment of a regimental badge atop the impressive nameplate. What wonderful machines and how powerful they seemed. Strangely enough 'Patriots' that happened along 'my line' were in the usual disreputable condition and I can well remember seeing No. 45501 several times before

realising that it was a 'namer', so insignificant and covered in grime was its *St. Dunstan's* nameplate as to render it virtually invisible.

Apart from leaning from a carriage window catching red hot 'smuts' in the eye the place *par excellence* to enjoy railway filth was the engine shed. This grubby environment was, of course, perfect for small, grubby boys and could have been made for them. Our parents were rarely in any doubt as to what we'd been up to and our arrival home must have been akin to welcoming a steam locomotive into the living room. Stations weren't the cleanest places on Earth either. We spent many hours waiting for trains and often entire nights at such beauty spots as Carlisle Citadel and Crewe, with the occasional carton of cold milk, from those vending machines that made a resounding 'thud', for sustenance. What a marvellous place Citadel was and what a great name for a station. The small hours produced a constant procession of sleeping car, parcels, mail and newspaper trains, many with top-link motive power, 'Duchesses', 'Scots', 'Jubes' and after 1963, 'Britannias'. 'Jinties' would fuss about as engines were changed and station staff would be busy loading and unloading parcels and mail. A few hours at such a place would permeate our clothes with an intoxicating sulphurous, sooty smell. I'm surprised that one of the famous perfume houses has not marketed an aerosol version of this.

Watching freight trains pass by presented other hazards, particularly on windy days. Cattle trains, coal trains, ore trains and so forth would leave their own distinctive aromas wafting around in the breeze, not to mention dust, long after their noisy passage.

The thought of freight trains brings forth many memories. My bedroom in Winson Green was directly opposite the railway embankment, which, as mentioned previously was mainly a goods line. The sound of clanking buffers and juddering brake levers accompanied my lapse in to the land of nod most nights.

Regular visits to steam centres for reference are an important part of my work and places like the Severn Valley Railway and the Great Central

Railway have a marvellous working atmosphere. The National Railway Museum at York is also an invaluable venue, although it would be marvellous if one of the turntables and its occupants could be allowed to 'weather' into a real working roundhouse to create the real feel of steam. Perhaps visitors could sign an indemnity form to relieve the museum of all liability for damage to clothes from oil and grease. It is interesting to note that some steam centres have recently allowed their engines and stock to become work-stained, realising perhaps that many of us prefer it that way. A greasy clean locomotive is far more convincing than one that has been cleaned to the point where it could be an ornament.

Adventures with cameras

As with many readers I suspect, one of my biggest regrets is not having a camera of any description during my younger years. Apart from the occasional holiday snap taken with the family box Brownie, which I always took charge of, the first time my trigger finger made the acquaintance of a shutter button was in 1961 when my grandad handed me a camera which he had scrounged from a rep' in his shop. The maker's name escapes me, but it was a nasty little plastic job, with matching lens, that used 620 film. We lived in Acocks Green at the time and at the first opportunity I was prowling around Tyseley sheds clicking away at everything in

sight. On the way home the film was handed into the local chemist and after the longest week, the results were collected with trepidation. Carefully taking the photographs from the neatly presented wallet must rate as one of the low points of my life. What greeted me was a set of grey, fuzzy, small square images which, on much closer inspection, were my carefully taken Tyseley shots. Certainly they were nothing at all like the Treacyesque pictures that were expected. It slowly dawned that my new camera was only remotely happy in bright sunlight with stationary objects and even then the definition was awful. Conditions at Tyseley had been quite beyond its capabilities.

There was no way that my paltry funds could afford a better camera and so for the next two years I persevered with the plastic job and consequently managed to produce just a handful of half reasonable pictures. Fate stepped in by depriving me of one grandmother, when my grandma Evans sadly died in 1963 and left each

of her grandchildren £15. This was a small fortune in those days and I knew exactly what to spend it on. During the two years of frustration with my awful camera I had got to know the local chemist, whose shop was partly devoted to camera equipment and accessories. He had been kind enough to teach me a thing or two about photography and now had a good idea of what I wanted. Many of my contemporaries were using Halina viewfinder cameras but, being naturally contrary my unexpected windfall was spent on a Voigtlander Vitoret, a fairly straightforward viewfinder camera with a top shutter speed of 1/125 of a second, a damned sight better than the 1/30 of a second that I had judged the old one to have, and a much better lens.

Tyseley once again was the first target where, it so happened that the following day promised to be, literally, quite special. A special train was due from Leeds and a 'Clan' Pacific was the planned motive power. So, on 26th March 1963, my brand new camera braced itself to record

A shot taken the day after buying a new camera, a Voigtlander Vitoret. This was about the fourth exposure on the first film and shows a rare visit by a 'Clan' Pacific to the Birmingham area when No. 72008 Clan Macleod *called at Tyseley on 26th March 1963 with a special train from Leeds. It later headed north with No. 7929* Wyke Hall *attached to the front as pilot. Other like-minded, camera toting characters can be seen plying their trade. The re-fuelling bays for DMUs are on the right and the shed yard and coaling plant on the left. (Author)*

A busy scene at Bournemouth Central taken with a second-hand Pentax SV with a 135mm lens attached, on 6th September 1966. Rebuilt 'West Country' Pacific No. 34100 Appledore is passing through with an up Channel Islands boat express while rebuilt 'Merchant Navy' No. 35027 Port Line waits at the platform with the up 'Royal Wessex'. My parents moved to Bournemouth in 1970 and I lived there, on and off, for a year or two. (Author)

accompany me to Scotland and several trips to the Southern Region where I enjoyed aiming the big lens at Bulleid Pacifics which seemed to lend themselves to the telephoto treatment. At the time I felt that the compression of perspective achieved by using this lens made these already puissant engines appear even more so. This particular piece of hardware became a firm favourite and in retrospect I probably used it far more than was necessary, or even sensible, and did so for many years. It still lurks in my camera case and occasionally comes out to play.

Photography in general became an important part of life throughout my college education and later led directly to landing a job as staff photographer with a local newspaper in 1970.

No. 72008 *Clan MacLeod* for posterity. The results were much more encouraging, the sun had shone for one thing, and these were the first of many that this camera was to take all over the country. Although, as with most of us it seems, the photographs were almost entirely locomotive portraits with the exclusion of practically every other facet of the railway. Such wasted opportunities which I'm probably still trying to make up for.

It soon became apparent that my new camera could not cope with fast moving trains, but again, lack of funds precluded any advancement in the technical department, although I did buy a second-hand enlarger and began to produce my own prints in a makeshift darkroom in the bathroom at first, much to mom's delight. Eventually, by 1966 I had saved enough money

to afford a second-hand Pentax and a 135 mm lens. Unfortunately this coincided with my declining interest in railways, but the camera did

A dramatically lit shed scene at Bournemouth taken on 21st January 1967 with the Pentax SV in low morning sunlight. 'West Country' Pacific No. 34001 Exeter with front numberplate missing, stands alongside Ivatt 2-6-2 tank No. 41295. (Author)

Shortly after realising that the 'Westerns' were still in existence this picture was taken at Penzance during the summer of 1973 whilst on holiday in St Ives. Another 135mm shot with the Pentax. (Author)

For some time the *Solihull News* had been using my sports pictures which I would shoot at weekends and deliver on Monday mornings. During one of these visits the editor invited me into his office and offered the position there and then. Apparently their regular photographer was away on long term sick leave and they were stuck. So began an interesting and enjoyable time shooting every sort of incident you could imagine. I soon learnt how to doctor the diary to make more of the work that interested me, such as fashion and sport, and less of the mundane presentations, openings and interminable civic functions involving the Mayor, whom I must have photographed hundreds of times. One memorable job involved a demonstration drive around the Rover cross-country test track in the newly introduced Range Rovers and another to cover a visit by Grace Kelly to open a fashion show.

In 1971 I became a freelance photographer for a while undertaking work for several newspapers and magazines, again specialising in sport, mainly football and rugby. Shortly afterwards marriage came along and the problem of where to live was solved with a job as an off-licence manager in Solihull which included living accommodation. The camera took a back seat for a while, only emerging to take family pictures. Railways hardly appeared in the viewfinder at all.

Cornwall was a regular holiday haunt and on our way to St Ives very early on a summer Saturday in 1973, we were stuck in the

I often find adverse weather conditions far more exciting than bright sunshine and much more of a challenge. This shot of a Class 47 heading an up East Coast express was taken at Retford on a foggy day in 1974. (Author)

A foul day at Newcastle Central in September 1976 surrounds the powerful image of 'Deltic' Class 55 No. 55022 Royal Scots Grey at rest after bringing in an express from King's Cross. Just prior to taking this photograph I had bent my car somewhat when I hit a concrete bollard in torrential rain by the railway at Gateshead. (Author)

traditional traffic jam on the A30 through Hayle – a by-pass has since been built. Nothing had moved for some considerable time and I found myself staring in a resigned way at the impressive viaduct leading into Hayle station when a train from Penzance came into view headed by No. 1073 *Western Bulwark*. Immediately my mind raced back to Tyseley bridge in 1962 when the 'Westerns' first appeared on the scene and I was quite taken aback to find them still intact – it now seemed such a long time ago. The following two weeks were spent taking photographs along the Plymouth to Penzance main line.

Thereafter, for the next three or four years, I made a point of getting out once a week whenever possible to photograph the current railway scene, soon getting into the swing of things again. Expeditions were planned with regard to weather, light and motive power, although this time my plan was to record more than just locomotives. My output was quite prolific for a time and regular batches of prints were submitted to Ian Allan Ltd and appeared, in some quantity in their publications, particularly *Modern Railways* where a couple of my photo-features were used – 'Brummy Freight' and 'Birmingham, Inter City Crossroads'. Regular visits were made to various locations on the East Coast Main Line to shoot the 'Deltics', and 'Westerns' suffered a similar fate, wherever they went.

I developed a style which tended towards low-key pictures which were often deliberately grainy. The mood and atmosphere of such offerings satisfied my sensibilities at the time and were the very opposite of the perfectly lit, pin-sharp record shots preferred by many enthusiasts with the result that a few derogatory letters came my way via the offices of Ian Allan Ltd. This only served to convince me that I must be doing something right!

The simple fact that I actually took all of those photographs, including those taken with my plastic camera, has proved to be a godsend to my work as an artist. Concerns about lighting conditions, angles and choosing a location are all to be considered when planning a painting, quite apart from their value as a straightforward record of course. It is vitally important to be aware of just what is involved when taking a photograph prior to using the information for a painting. Mistakes and misrepresentations are all too easy to make when data is translated onto canvas by the ill-informed artist. The effect of lenses of different focal lengths must be understood thoroughly. An image taken through a telephoto, for example, when transferred to the foreground of a painting will appear to be 'wrong'. Conversely an image through a wide-angle lens used in the background will also appear to be out of place. Only once have I used all the elements of a photograph in a painting and in this case it was a combination of two exposures.

I have mentioned before that photographs are a vital ingredient to any artist depicting the steam age and when working on a canvas I am usually surrounded by dozens of them, not all totally relevant to the work in hand, but which may have a flavour of my intentions. The camera is an important part of my armoury even when dealing with contemporary subjects and is a convenient way to gather reference material quickly and as a back-up to any drawings and sketches that may be made at the same time. Many artists tend to become secretive when questioned about the use of photographs, feeling perhaps that the employment of such things would be considered as cheating by somehow short-cutting the perceived traditional artistic process. Long before the invention of the camera many of the great masters used a form of epidiascope to record complex scenes. Giovanni Canaletto for example, achieved his remarkable views of Venice in the 18th century by using such a system to establish the basic drawing and to ascertain the effect of shadows and so forth.

An awful lot of nonsense is spoken when the relative merits of photography and paintings as artforms are discussed. Both produce pictures but a snapshot is a world apart from a skilfully executed and well considered photograph taken by an artistic cameraman. A picture is a picture whatever method is used to create it and surely the viewer can decide whether it is art or not.

Since the end of steam on British Railways in 1968 only a handful of photographs of steam specials have emerged from my cameras. The whole carnival that surrounds these trains is the exact antithesis of what I enjoy about railways. The day in day out aspect of the railway, locomotives working, simply doing their job, hauling passengers and freight in all conditions is what appeals to me, not a highly polished one-off event surrounded by thousands of camera-clad individuals fighting for the best view. This may sound uncharitable to the efforts of preservation societies, but it is most certainly not intended to be. Many preserved lines are terrific and some are mentioned elsewhere in these pages.

Making a living

My interest in art increased during my time at Lordswood Technical School and was encouraged by two teachers, Mr Rankin and the appropriately named Mr Hart. Another subject which intrigued me was technical drawing. I enjoyed using pens, pencils, brushes, clay and so forth to create something from nothing whereas some other subjects, particularly chemistry, filled me with dread. Each time I crossed the threshold of the chemistry laboratory it was as though a portcullis dropped around my brain allowing no sensible thought to escape. By comparison, the freedom of the artroom seemed like heaven.

During a parents' evening in my fourth year my parents were told by the art teachers that perhaps teaching, particularly art, could be my forte and the T.D. teacher, Mr Harrington, informed them that I was excellent design draughtsman material. Both of these careers obviously appealed to them with mom being particularly smitten by the former idea. Unfortunately I had other plans. The only thing in my mind was to go to art college at the earliest opportunity, but this desire was kept under wraps until the last minute when the time came for them to sign the necessary forms. They were a little disappointed perhaps, particularly mom, but gave their consent willingly.

The course chosen at Birmingham College of Art & Design was a pre-diploma one-year stretch which was designed to give students a taste of each of the diploma subjects which could be pursued full-time for the remaining three years. These included fine art, graphic design, industrial design, dress design, photography and so forth. Fine art was my choice from the beginning but it quickly became apparent that any tendency towards representational work was frowned upon. Apart from life drawing classes very little else made sense. Being given a number of straight lines and filling space meaningfully with them was not exactly what I had in mind. Had I been a little older and more mature my reaction may have been very different but in my rush to get to art college I had left school after taking 'O' levels whereas most of the other students had stayed on for their 'A' levels. Nevertheless I persevered and recall vividly a particular tutor's reactions when a group of us returned from a drawing session in the city centre. On seeing my drawing of New Street station in the early stages of reconstruction he wasted no time in informing one and all that this is exactly what we should *not* be doing, preferring instead, other more esoteric offerings. Disillusioned but undaunted I completed the year only to discover that I was too young to begin a diploma course and would have to repeat the exercise or apply for a vocational course. The thought of another year with unsympathetic tutors held absolutely no appeal and so I enquired about the alternatives. The only course that seemed vaguely to suit my needs was technical illustration, and in September 1965 I embarked on three years of training to produce elaborate perspective drawings, discover the

The author with Standard tank armrest at the Severn Valley Railway, 1998. (Ben Hawkins)

During a visit in 1971 I discovered that there was a regular open air exhibition of paintings in the winter gardens, where, for a nominal fee, it was possible to rent a few square feet of hanging space. A few watercolours and drawings were quickly produced and sold. Although the prices were extremely modest I enjoyed the feeling.

One incident from this venue sticks in my mind. A local gentleman had spent a long time gazing at my work and eventually asked if I had ever painted the 'Bournemouth Belle' in Bournemouth Central station. 'Funny you should ask that', I replied, 'the picture you describe is back at my studio and I could bring it tomorrow for you to see!' This was not strictly true of course, but as usual I was in need of funds and returned quickly to my parents' home, gathered together a few materials and reference, and worked through the night on the 'Bournemouth Belle'. A frame and mount were taken from another picture and next morning, bright and breezy, I appeared at the winter gardens, having the brand new watercolour complete with a 'reserve' ticket and sat back in the sunshine feeling pleased with myself. My would-be patron duly turned up, was delighted with the picture and bought it there and then. The exact price escapes me but it would have been between £25 and £40 for the modestly proportioned painting.

Highly unethical perhaps but extremely satisfying, and my first commission. I haven't seen the painting in question from that day to this and would no doubt be horrified if I did, but I was delighted with it at the time and definitely enjoyed the experience. In fact, this incident probably hardened my resolve to earn a living from painting.

At this time I was earning a crust from freelance photography and selling the odd painting, although my income from the latter

delights of annotations, cut-away sections, exploded views, lettering and airbrush. Not really what I had intended to do but my fellow students were great company and some remain good friends to this day.

At this time students were virtually guaranteed a good job at the end of the course and I was offered a position at Metro-Cammell, Washwood Heath, not far from home. The fact that this company was well known, and still are, for producing railway locomotives and rolling stock amongst other things, was quite coincidental as was the fact that dad had been a coach-trimmer there before and after the war. As the company had never employed a technical illustrator before there was some uncertainty about my role. This suited me fine and I was able to create needs which they had never realised existed and produced artist's impressions of

locomotives for Malawi and Pakistan and of proposed London Underground stock, oil tankers and containers amongst other things, working from blue-prints supplied by the army of draughtsmen. After a year or so of this enjoyable employment design and production of new rolling stock began to slow down, consequently the need for my artist's impressions subsided likewise and I found myself having to produce technical illustrations almost exclusively. This aspect of the work was less appealing and, having no commitments at this time, I handed in my notice and became a freelance photographer. Throughout my stay at Metro-Cammell I produced a few paintings, mainly water colour, some of railway subjects and managed to sell most of them.

In the summer of 1970 my parents moved to Bournemouth and I visited them quite often.

was minute. Nevertheless the desire to paint full-time was strong. For as long as I could remember paintings of all types had fascinated me. Cuneo's pictures on BR posters and model railway catalogues, amongst other things, grabbed my attention and during 1969, give or take a year or two, there was an exhibition of the man's railway work in the foyer of the *Birmingham Post & Mail* building in the city centre and many hours were spent pouring over them. Likewise a small exhibition of the wonderful work of J. M. W. Turner at the Birmingham City Art Gallery found me gazing in awe. One painting in particular, 'Coniston Water', encompassed everything that I felt a work of art should be, it was lyrical, vital, dripping in mood and atmosphere and so beautifully executed. Some time was spent considering the best way to remove it from the gallery without being noticed. These experiences and countless others determined my desire to play a part in the world of art, however small.

Meanwhile, real life took over. As previously mentioned, marriage came along in November 1971 and the problem of somewhere to live was solved by taking a job as an off-licence manager for Mitchells & Butlers in Solihull. In spite of the unsociable hours, Cath and I coped easily with the task, leaving time to devote to painting. From about 1975 customers were treated to a display of four or five paintings, mainly of railway subjects, and for the first time I was struck by how many were interested in trains; all types of people. Amongst those who showed an interest was Bernard Apps, now my Quicksilver Publishing partner.

At this time my paintings were framed at a small gallery in nearby Dorridge, called Garrett Fine Arts. The owner John Letts, a well-known Midlands' sculptor, kindly offered to organise an exhibition of my work during the spring of 1977. This comprised a dozen or so paintings and drawings and there was some useful local press coverage and public reaction was very encouraging resulting in most of the work being sold.

Later the same year we moved to a private house complete with mortgage. The move was far from straightforward because of the nature of my job although this was resolved when I negotiated a new position in the display department of the same brewery. Unfortunately, shortly after moving, this new job fell through, as apparently the director who had authorised my appointment had had a disagreement with the company and left under a cloud. So, we had a new house, a new mortgage and a new son Ben, but no 'proper' employment. Christmas was approaching fast and I became a milkman for a while, which of course included the financial boost of festive tips. I'm afraid I found the job loathsome and couldn't wait to complete my round each day. The soul purpose of the work seemed to revolve around getting back to the depot and then home as quickly as possible. My resignation was handed in a week into the new year, so ending the shortest career in the milk delivery business.

Perhaps the move to become a full-time painter should have been made much earlier but I was always mindful of my family's opinions and the advice of others who had continually warned of the possible pitfalls of trying to earn a living in this way. Also they were definitely of the opinion that painting was not a 'proper job'. Nevertheless the thought of reaching old age and wondering what might have happened had I taken the plunge was beginning to haunt me and the feeling that I could make a go of it was strong. Consequently, during the summer of 1978, much to the dismay of family and friends I entered the precarious world of the self-employed artist.

The problem of where to work was solved quite by chance when I called to see John Letts at his new studio in Shirley, Solihull. Not long before, he had moved into a group of garages which had been knocked into one and converted into offices. John was using these premises as a modelling studio and workshop but had a couple of rooms doing very little. He immediately offered the use of these rooms for a nominal rent and I moved in. Part of one room was partitioned off to form a darkroom and another

became my studio. This was to be my workplace for the next six years and most congenial it was too. John is one of the kindest, most generous people it has been my good fortune to meet and, amongst other things, kept me supplied with cigarettes and newspapers. The only thing I could afford to give in return were my old brushes which were employed to fill awkward corners of rubber moulds used to produce his limited edition sculptures.

Making any sort of living proved to be extremely difficult and the dire warnings of the doubters came back to haunt me on many occasions and still do, but occasionally things went well enough to bolster my spirits. To enable us to function as a family – eat, pay the bills and keep the building society happy – Cath took some lousy jobs to supplement my meagre earnings. Sadly, we are no longer together but her help and encouragement during those difficult years are remembered with deep gratitude.

From the start I specialised in railway paintings simply because that was what I knew and loved, but never thinking that sufficient work would come my way to remain in this field until the present time. Occasionally I would paint other subjects but as more railway work was undertaken I began to realise what a vast subject this was. Some commissions opened new doors, particularly historic and foreign subjects, enabling me to research hitherto unknown areas.

In 1984 we decided to convert the loft at home into a studio so ending my 'garage' period. Once again a prerequisite was that there should be a darkroom and with some canny planning this was organised across the landing from my new studio. Much has happened since then but at the time of writing it is still my base.

Today, 75 per cent of my output is to commission but in the early days it was a case of selling paintings wherever and however I could. Galleries proved to be very hit and miss, seldom buying work outright and sometimes very reluctant to pay promptly after selling work left on a sale or return basis. Another annoying aspect was that they rarely kept a promise to inform me of the whereabouts of any pictures sold, with the result that I have effectively lost contact with them for future reference. For a few years John Letts and I staged regular exhibitions at the Solihull library gallery, usually during November and December. This proved to be an effective combination with John's sculptures occupying the floor space whilst my work hung on the walls. Several commissions came my way from these occasions and slowly but surely patrons of my particular art materialised to the extent that now I have some two year's commissioned work ahead.

Some people may be upset by the following remark, but painting for a living is much the same as any other business. Unless prospective clients see the work of an artist then they will never know that it exists. With painting the obvious solution to this problem is publishing in its many and varied forms. We are surrounded in our day to day life with printed images of all types, many of them derived from paintings, on anything from tablemats to advertisement hoardings and every conceivable item in between. Whatever an artist's speciality there is usually a commercial outlet to suit and with railway art these are probably more clearly defined than with some other subjects.

The urgency to see one's work in print can easily cloud considered judgement when discussing and considering publishing deals, resulting in the artist signing over all-time, worldwide copyright for very little financial return thereby handing the publisher carte blanche to use the work in any way they think fit, and make a profit into the bargain. In 1979, I was approached by a major London fine art publisher who was keen to reproduce a painting as a fine art print. Obviously this was very flattering and I duly signed an agreement without taking much

notice of the small print, which I later discovered signed over all my rights to the picture. My reproduction fee, the going rate for the time, was for use of the painting as a fine art print, or so I thought. Over the next two or three years it appeared as a jigsaw and a gift token card with no further fee forthcoming. Great care has been

taken when signing agreements and contracts since, but no doubt mistakes will always be made. At about the same time one or two less than ideal publishing arrangements were entered into with the resultant prints not living up to expectations by a mile. . . Still, we live and learn and gradually, by trial and error, listening to good advice and bitter experience I became more aware of how to guard against such spurious deals and I'm still learning!

To date my work has been used for greetings cards, collectors' plates, calendars, fine art prints and in books, newspapers and magazines. One of

the most constant and rewarding associations has been with Eversheds the well-known calendar and diary publishers. Jim Wilson, then a director of the company, approached me in 1984 with a view to producing a set of six pictures for use in the 1986 advertising calendar to be known as *Footplate*. I've no idea how he got to know my work but he obviously liked what he saw and so began a happy relationship that continues to this day, in fact recently, the pictures for the 1999 *Footplate* calendar were delivered. This will be the 14th year, making a total of 84 paintings!

It is often said that a creative temperament is not compatible with sound business sense and, although I've muddled along fairly well, I have always found the selling side of things distasteful. Perhaps I cope better nowadays but can still become quite embarrassed when showered with praise, particularly when offered in a patronising manner. Genuine criticism I enjoy and can handle much better. Perhaps we all need someone who has opposing business attributes and that someone came my way in the shape of Bernard Apps, a long-time acquaintance and now good friend and publishing partner. Together, we are Quicksilver Publishing, a business formed in 1988 to publish, promote and sell fine art prints of my paintings. We have long term plans to publish the works of other artists, not only those specialising in railways. The only proviso being that the work has to be excellent. Bernard, a self-confessed Philistine, is rapidly learning the finer points of art appreciation. Whether I am doing likewise with the business aspects of things is debatable!

The thrill of seeing my work in print never wanes and the fact that many more people can see, enjoy and own copies of my paintings in this way gives me great pleasure.

Philip Hawkins

The Paintings

Thornbury Castle

Wolverhampton Stafford Road sheds have been mentioned earlier and '**Thornbury Castle**', commissioned by Pete Waterman for the Waterman Railways Heritage Trust, was a great excuse to put memories into practice. Pete had been a boiler fitters apprentice at 84A in the late 1950s and remembers the place, warts and all, with much affection. Additionally, he had recently acquired No. 7027, which had languished at Tyseley for many years and plans to restore the engine to working order – no mean feat! Consequently there was absolutely no question over the location for the picture. The year is 1959 and No. 7027 was allocated to Old Oak Common and would have worked into Wolverhampton Low Level with a train from Paddington before adjourning to Stafford Road for servicing. This was a truly filthy place with many of the ancient buildings in a dangerous, dilapidated state. The 'Castle' is in a condition that I often refer to as 'greasy clean', not perfect but pretty damned good. This makes a pointed contrast with the squalid location, and a 'Modified Hall' buffered up to 7027 is in a condition known locally as 'Stafford Road green'. When the completed work was delivered to Pete at the Crewe Heritage Centre he showed me around the loco which was being dismantled. Parts stamped with the numbers of several other

Another "Castle"

'Castles' were amongst those already removed – fascinating eh!

A clear childhood memory is seeing the first double-chimney 'Castle', No. 7018 *Drysllwyn Castle*, or 'Drizzling Castle' as we called it! The year was 1956 and it was in spanking condition with the number clearly visible from my 'pitch' between the bridges. At last, I thought, the Western was catching up with the lovely chimneys seen every day on the London, Midland 'Scots'. To me the 'Castles' looked fine with this carbuncle, as described by many. An overabundance of perfection can be a little tedious and these chimneys gave, what was already one of my favourite classes, an edge over the ordinary members. What No. 7018, a Bristol Bath Road engine at the time, was doing in this neck of the woods I do not know, but it hung around for several days and became a firm favourite. Possibly it was running trials. In more recent years it has been strange to see the preserved No. 5051 running with *Drysllwyn Castle* nameplates, quite properly of course. At that time we knew this engine as *Earl Bathurst* and in fact, No. 7018 was the third wearer of the plates. The other had been No. 5076, which they graced from 1937 until 1941.

Thornbury Castle (1996)
Oil on Canvas 30" x 20"

Birmingham New Street/The Midlander

Private collection: *USA.*

Birmingham New Street (1985)
Oil on Canvas 20" x 16"

In '**Birmingham New Street**' I have attempted to portray the atmosphere of my 'second home'. The engine is 'Patriot' 4-6-0 No. 45506 *The Royal Pioneer Corps* which is standing at Platform 7 with a train from its home city of Bristol which will be going on to Sheffield, York or Newcastle. It is 1959/60 and the time is soon after midday with shafts of sunlight forcing a way through the smoke and steam to create the sort of 'light cocktail' that today's photographers of preserved steam would kill for. The painting is now in a private collection in the USA.

'**The Midlander**' is a view of New Street from near my 'spot' on Platform 6 and features a 'Jubilee' 4-6-0, No. 45688 *Polyphemus*, running in from Euston in the mid '50s. The train is composed of ex LMS stock but painted in BR's 'blood & custard' livery. In the background, at Platform 3, a Fowler 2-6-4 tank is waiting to leave with a local train, perhaps for Lichfield, while a 'Black 5' has its thirst quenched at Platform 1. I must have seen *Polyphemus* hundreds of times. Throughout most of the '50s it was one of Bushbury's stud of 'Jubilees' and never wandered far from the Wolverhampton, Birmingham and Euston route. The 'Midlander' headboard seemed to be a permanent fixture. This painting was commissioned by Mr Andrew Harper, another 'Brummie' who also has the same fond memories of his favourite station as I. Interestingly the retaining wall, behind the engine, and some of the red brick buildings still remain to confine the present day concrete New Street. The Rotunda now dominates the centre background and the distinctive Worcester Street buildings above the signalbox disappeared during the rebuilding in 1964. With a generous helping of imagination it is just possible to picture this scene today, if you can ignore the plethora of overhead catenary equipment.

The sulphurous confines of New Street station were divided into two distinct sections, the London & North Western side and the Midland Railway side. This historical division was perpetuated by the LMS with ex LNWR and MR engines rarely straying over the 'fence'. When I became intimately involved with the place in the fifties, this apartheid was a little less pronounced but nevertheless the distinctive character remained. Trainspotters of the period would gather at two particular vantage points to be sure of seeing everything that slipped into and out of every platform. The east (London) end of Platform 6 was the favourite spot. There was rarely a dull moment and always the possibility that something 'rare' would show up. The old Midland side still retained its, by then, dilapidated overall roof and always seemed to smell of fish.

Collection: *Andrew Harper Esq.*

The Midlander (1992)
Oil on Canvas 30" x 20"

New Street 1957

Following the success of 'On Time' in 1985, the *Birmingham Post & Mail* decided to commission another painting the following year, again with a view to offering fine art prints to their many readers. The obvious choice was, of course, New Street station as a companion to Snow Hill.

odd planks missing

lamps, notices, etc supported thus

Detail of roof structure & pillar.

Being aware that in the popularity stakes New Street trailed behind its Great Western competitor by about 2 to 1, I clearly saw the task as having to produce something which would have at least as much appeal to the *Post & Mail* readers as 'On Time'. Early on, the period decided upon was to be the 1950s and that it had to be the old Midland Railway side of the station because I loved the dilapidated grandeur of that crumbling roof and the curves of the platforms. Also, I knew that there was no better time to be there than on a Bank Holiday when there always seemed to be trains queuing to get in and out.

So, the scene was set in my mind's eye, there just remained the rather daunting task of gathering the appropriate reference material. Here, the newspaper's photo library proved to be a gold mine of wonderfully evocative pictures, even of holiday crowds. Little by little, information was gathered. The locomotives were to be a 'Patriot', No. 45509 *The Derbyshire Yeomanry*, a Derby engine at this time and one frequently seen at New Street, and a 'Jubilee', No. 45682 *Trafalgar*, a Bristol Barrow Road engine and a 'crate' if ever there was one during my childhood. The roof, if anything, looks far grander than it actually was and if I were to repeat the exercise the 'dad and son' in the foreground would be sent back along the platform to concentrate the eye more on the locomotives and to emphasise their size. The composition is similar to 'The Bristolian', reproduced later in the book, and which had

Light

Red tie

Show sharp creases with plenty of material.

Grey

turn-ups.

Group for platform 10.

many of the same problems.

A mistake was made in the caption on the print of this painting by stating that it was August Bank holiday 1957 and I duly received a letter, a long letter, from a diligent gentleman who had made complete records of all workings on the Derby–Birmingham–Bristol route during the '50s. He was absolutely certain that the two engines would not have been seen together at New Street on this particular day, although they were both working on this line. Oh well! You can please some of the people etc, etc. The print did sell as anticipated – half as well as 'On Time'!

Grandma complete with luggage - on Platform 9

Blue

Standing in front of loco 45682.

Cream

Basket with flask in view

Blue

Smarties

Brown

Green Shirt

Grey flannel

9th July '86

right foreground, perhaps with suitcase.

New Street 1957 (1986)
Oil on Canvas 30" x 24"

On Time

The 150th anniversary of the Great Western Railway stimulated the *Birmingham Post & Mail* to commission a painting to commemorate the event in 1985. For obvious reasons a picture with very apparent local interest was required in order to whet the appetite of readers when the time came to promote fine art prints of the painting. There was really no contest – it just had to be Snow Hill station. That was the easy part, the rest was up to me. After considering various periods, locomotive types and trains, not to mention such things as viewpoints and angles, I decided upon the year 1947, the last before Nationalisation. The viewpoint had to be one that, although immediately recognisable, hadn't been 'done to death' in the railway press, particularly in fine art print form. After travelling in my time-machine around every nook and cranny of the station on which so much time had been spent as a kid, I settled on a view that would prominently feature one of the famous clocks. Now, as one of these was overlooking the concourse it had to be the one on Platform 7, the London side. It was only after making these seemingly logical decisions that I discovered that practically no photographs had been taken from anything

" Station Master
Mr Arthur Hammond Elsden "

like this angle and so the whole had to be worked out from scratch. Eventually the basic drawing was made featuring a 'King', No. 6008 *King James II,* on the midday Paddington train. The view chosen gave prominence to the initials GW on the tender and this, together with the clock and general impression of the station gave no doubt as to what and where it was. My son Ben is the lad seated on the suitcase and I was able to include an impression of the then stationmaster, Arthur Hammond Emsden, to add to the period atmosphere – he was quite a character I understand. Local railway historian Derek Harrison provided some useful reference for this work.

All in all a rather complicated picture to bring together but the effort was well rewarded when the first print run sold out within two months of the newspaper promotion. It was ultimately reprinted twice and has since been republished by Quicksilver Publishing. This picture involved me in a most unusual 'print signing' session when, on the occasion of the re-opening of Snow Hill Tunnel, I was asked by the *Post & Mail* to

sign copies for 'tunnel walkers' when they emerged into the new station after walking in the darkness from Moor Street. This one-off event was organised by the *Evening Mail* with donations from the £1 'walker's fee' going to local charities. An amazing 14,057 people made the walk on 12th September 1987 and I was signing prints constantly for the entire day. Tracks were laid through the tunnel and the station opened in the spring of 1988.

'Young fireman taking
a breather'

On Time (1985)
Oil on Canvas 30" x 20"

Night Wolf/Flying Fox – Flying/Pacific Parade

Pacific Parade (1984)
Oil on Canvas 20" x 16"

Flying Fox – Flying (1997)
Oil on Panel 15" x 12"

'**Night Wolf**' is a moody portrait of one of Edward Thompson's A2/2 Pacifics near the end of its days at New England shed, Peterborough. These engines were rebuilt by Thompson from Nigel Gresley's impressive P2 2-8-2s, a deed which has been covered at great length by many commentators, mostly in a derogatory vein. I took an immediate liking to these monstrous machines on seeing a photograph in a friend's ABC when still quite young. I recall seeing three of them at Doncaster in 1959, but as far as I can recollect the only one seen in steam was No. 60506 *Wolf of Badenoch* at New England late in 1960 not long before withdrawal in April 1961. Its condition in the painting is as I remember and was the only one never to have beading added to its stove-pipe chimney. What a wonderful name for a steam locomotive!

Am I alone in being quite partial to A3s in their final form with double chimneys and German type deflectors? These appendages gave an otherwise beautifully balanced, finely proportioned machine a slightly front-heavy appearance resulting in a rather odd look, which I quite liked. In recent years it has been a treat to see *Flying Scotsman* in this guise. My intentions in '**Flying Fox – Flying**' were quite straightforward, simply to show off the graceful lines whilst speeding along the East Coast Main Line – just as Sir Nigel intended. No. 60106 was not withdrawn until December 1964 and attained the highest mileage of its class.

As already mentioned, my first sight of an A4 Pacific, in the flesh, was at King's Cross station after persuading dad to make a detour on our way to the Motor Show at Earl's Court, an annual treat. The year must have been 1958 or maybe 1959. '**Pacific Parade**' depicts the period just prior to this before the A4s were fitted with double chimneys, apart from the four so built of course. The country end of Platform 10 was a mecca for train watchers from nine to 90 with generation after generation gathering to witness spectacles such as this, all for free! A4 No. 60015 *Quicksilver* is taking off with the 'Tees-Tyne Pullman' whilst a Peppercorn A1 Pacific, No. 60131 *Osprey*, waits impatiently to follow on with an express for Leeds and Bradford. At the time of writing, work is well underway to construct one of these handsome engines from the original blueprints. It is to be No. 60163 *Tornado*.

Night Wolf (1986)
Oil on Canvas 20" x 16"

Waiting in the Night/Night Call/Night Freight

Collection: *David Asbury Esq.*

Collection: *David Asbury Esq.*

Night Call (1993)
Oil on Board 12" x 10"

Night Freight (1994)
Oil on Canvas 20" x 16"

There is something quite intoxicating about the railway at night and this feeling is intensified where steam locomotives are involved. When very young I would lie in bed watching the orange firebox glow and leaping sparks passing to and fro the bedroom window, the crew silhouetted against the glare from the footplate, the fireman hard at work with the shovel, coaxing their steed to the top of the bank. From an artistic viewpoint I am sure that several 'old masters' would have had a field day with this most evocative of subjects.

'**Waiting in the Night**' portrays a Stanier 8F 2-8-0, No. 48197, waiting for the road in Washwood Heath yards, Birmingham not long before the end of steam working in this area. It was always a wonder how the little engineman's hut remained upright on each subsequent visit as a few more bricks seemed to have disappeared!

Throughout my career there have been periods

when I would concentrate on specific themes, trains in snow leaps to mind, but I return time and again to the nocturnal scene, never trains flashing through the countryside, although that is a thought, but rather the locomotive in repose, simmering quietly to itself and emitting all manner of bronchial sounds, or like a coiled spring impatient to be on the move. '**Night Call**' falls into the latter category. A rebuilt 'West Country' Pacific, No. 34028 *Eddystone*, waits impatiently at Bournemouth Central station while station staff go about their business before the train continues its journey to Weymouth. This picture is based on a photograph taken by myself in 1964. It was a time exposure and as I had no tripod at the time various items of luggage were carefully stacked onto a luggage trolley to fashion a suitable resting place for my camera. The result still suffered from camera shake! Bournemouth Central became quite well

known to me during the first half of the 1960s, often hopping off the train, 'bunking' the shed, then back on to the next departure to Weymouth or Eastleigh, depending on my itinerary.

In '**Night Freight**' a low viewpoint was deliberately chosen to emphasis the massive proportions of these imposing engines. No. 4706, allocated to Bristol St Philip's Marsh, waits noisily on the goods avoiding lines at Exeter St Davids with a down fitted freight, c1960. I particularly enjoy 'low key' pictures and try to take advantage of the situation to use points of light and highlights to take the eye for a wander around the scene. It is important for me to create a sense of being able to walk around the back of the train to discover what may be there and to summon an air of mystery as the train disappears into the distance, a mixture of smoke, steam and the night.

Waiting in the Night (1989)
Oil on Canvas 20" x 16"

Island Summer/Evercreech Junction

Collection: *Private.*

Evercreech Junction (1989)
Oil on Canvas 30" x 20"

Although my prime interest has veered towards busy city railways and main line engines I do appreciate the quieter charms of country branch lines and by-ways and, of course, the locomotives, rolling stock and architecture often have a character that is food and drink to an artist. There is certainly enormous enthusiasm for such lines, witness the number of books on individual branch lines that have been published in recent years, often written by enthusiasts who have spent a lifetime researching their subject. To many, the branch line is the epitome of a British railway, conjuring up, as it does, the rural idyll to which many of us seemingly aspire.

'**Island Summer**' was painted for purely selfish reasons. During the mid 1950s, for three or four years on the trot, I holidayed with my grandparents at Ryde on the Isle of Wight. We stayed at the Marine Hotel which happened to be directly opposite Ryde pier. How grandad could afford the luxury of a fortnight at such a palace was a mystery. Nothing else, at this time, approached the grandeur of this summer holiday! Our room and the dining room overlooked a constant procession of O2-hauled trains packed to overflowing with holiday-makers. To a small boy used to a steady diet of 'Scots' and 'Jubes' the tiny tank engines made quite an impression, particularly when working bunker first back to Ryde. During these holidays I don't ever remember actually travelling by train but rectified this in the early '60s, making several visits and in the process discovered Ventnor station. What an amazing place this was. The approach, through a barely adequate tunnel, opened out into a neat station surrounded by chalk cliffs dotted with caves. One of the two platforms was isolated from the 'Way Out' by running tracks and required a 'bridge' to be manhandled into position between these platforms to allow the eager throngs loose into Ventnor town. The engine, incidentally, is No. 24 *Calbourne*.

Summer Saturday traffic was the lifeblood of '**Evercreech Junction**' and the Somerset & Dorset railway in general, particularly in the 1950s. Indeed, mass motor car ownership was probably the main reason for the line's eventual demise in 1966 with dwindling returns on passenger receipts overtaking the line's *raison d'etre*.

Thanks to the marvellous photographs and wonderfully evocative cine film taken by the late Ivo Peters, the delights of the S&D are known and loved far and wide. My own recollections are of several visits to Bath engine shed and a couple of trips along the line, once behind a Saltley 'Black 5' throughout from Birmingham New Street to Bath and then a Standard Class 5 on to Bournemouth, in 1964 I think.

The S&D's 2-8-0s were fascinating engines and, to my eyes, quite unlike anything else. The fact that they were regularly employed on passenger trains only added to their appeal. For my painting I chose to feature one of the preserved engines, No. 53808, with one of the line's 4-4-0s, No. 40700. Approaching is an unrebuilt 'West Country', No. 34043 *Combe Martin* with a train load of returning holiday-makers. The year is 1960 and in just a few years the line and the station would be gone for ever. Incidentally, the engineman leaning against the water crane is from a drawing made on the Severn Valley Railway some years ago. They all come in handy, sooner or later!

Island Summer (1991)
Oil on Canvas 20" x 16"

Bordesley Morning/Rush Hour at Rubery

Collection: *Mrs 'Tot' Clarke.*

Rush Hour at Rubery (1982)
Oil on Canvas 30" x 20"

'Rush Hour at Rubery' evoked similar memories for John Clarke of Birmingham who commissioned this painting based on a photograph by the late Peter Shoesmith. John had spent most of his working life at the Austin factory at Longbridge and remembered the workman's special trains that ran from here to Halesowen. The year is 1947 and pannier No. 7402, another Tyseley inmate, is running through Rubery with one of these trains. The ex Midland Railway Class 2F 0-6-0 in the distance is a reminder that the line was a joint MR and GWR venture.

"RUSH HOUR AT RUBERY"

The everyday comings and goings of local freight trains and shunting engines was so commonplace that very few of us even bothered to take a glance, and of all the locomotive types of my childhood, Great Western pannier tanks, or 'matchboxes' as we irreverantly called them, were the most common bar none and could be seen scurrying by at any time of day at the bottom of my road. Most of the local ones were based at Tyseley sheds. No. 4648 in 'Bordesley Morning' is no exception and is seen here approaching Bordesley station along the down main line in charge of a northbound transfer freight, probably bound for Hockley yards just north of Birmingham Snow Hill. Bordesley was the first stop out of Snow Hill heading south along the GW main line to Paddington. The bridge in the background carries the Midland Railway Camp Hill freight line which enabled trains on the Bristol to Derby line, heading north also to avoid the bottleneck of New Street station. This scene, apart from a few missing tracks and signals is remarkably intact even today, including the Great Western warehouse seen in the right background.

Collection: *David Asbury Esq.*

Bordesley Morning (1997)
Oil on Panel 15" x 12"

51

Duchess of the Night/Rushing Through Rugeley

Collection: *Gordon Barker Esq.*

Rushing Through Rugeley (1985)
Oil on Canvas 30" x 20"

These paintings show William Stanier's magnificent 'Princess Coronation' Pacifics at opposite ends of their careers. **'Duchess of the Night'** features No. 46228 *Duchess of Rutland* awaiting the rightaway from Rugby Midland station on a murky, smokey winter evening with a Wolverhampton–Birmingham New Street–London Euston train in 1963. After a lifetime working crack expresses up and down the West Coast Main Line these fabulous engines were usurped from 1959/60 by the English Electric Type 4s (later Class 40s) and found themselves relegated to lesser duties such as that shown here, much to the delight of 'Brummie' spotters who hitherto had to rely upon Sunday diversions through the city to see the 'Semies'. No. 46228 was built at Crewe in 1938 as a streamliner, defrocked in 1947 and withdrawn from service in September 1964. Hardly a long life but a glorious one!

In **'Rushing Through Rugeley'** No. 6230 *Duchess of Buccleuch* is seen in the first flush of youth roaring along the West Coast Main Line approaching Rugeley Trent Valley with a Euston–Glasgow express just prior to the Second World War. This engine was the first of the class to be built non-streamlined and is portrayed as originally built in June 1938 with a single chimney. As a resident of Polmadie depot, Glasgow throughout the 1950s until withdrawal in November 1963, No. 46230 as I knew it, was a rarity to us kids in Birmingham although I did see it at Crewe during 1960. In the form shown here the 'Duchesses' were considered by many observers to be the epitomy of British steam locomotive design, both in appearance and performance. They were certainly handsome machines.

Duchess of the Night (1996)
Oil on Canvas 20" x 16"

Southern Freeze/Southern Sunset

Collection: *Artist's.*

Southern Sunset (1997)
Oil on Canvas 15" x 12"

preservation. Some two years after the painting was completed, published and sold a letter arrived from a well-meaning critic to inform me that the tender is of the wrong pattern for this particular engine at this time. He was quite correct! This is a cautionary tale for all railway artists when working from scraps of reference: be very careful when changing numbers of locomotives among other things! The mistake was particularly annoying because I had made a note regarding the tender early on in the proceedings.

Another Bulleid Light Pacific, this time a 'West Country', No. 34002 *Salisbury*, features in **'Southern Sunset'**, hard at work on the LSWR main line in charge of an Exeter–Waterloo express climbing the 1 in 90 gradient of Honiton bank in Devon approaching the tunnel. Quite a straightforward picture with the telegraph poles marching alongside the down line forming a crucial part of the composition.

Both of these paintings were completed for inclusion in the appropriate section of calendars. 'Southern Freeze' was a long time in the planning stage. The locomotive was no problem and the choice of location was easy, but I particularly wanted to dwell upon the contrast of the arctic conditions with the warmth of the fires, both on the footplate and the brazier. Calculating the angles to show these elements to satisfaction

took some time before deciding on the final composition. Reference for Exmouth Junction shed was also surprisingly shy at the time. Quite a complex picture in some ways but the research and planning paid off with the execution presenting few problems. The harsh winter of 1963 is the period and the locomotive a Bulleid 'Battle of Britain' Pacific, No. 34072 *257 Squadron*, one of 20 such engines to survive into

Collection: *Roy Apps Esq.*

Southern Freeze (1985)
Oil on Canvas 20" x 16"

Firth of Forth/Shrewsbury Standard/Iron Duke and the Shed Cat

Collection: *David Asbury Esq.*

Shrewsbury Standard (1994)
Oil on Canvas 20" x 16"

Collection: *David Asbury Esq.*

Iron Duke and the Shed Cat (1991)
Oil on Canvas 20" x 16"

'**Firth of Forth**' was commissioned by Mr Bob Robson who has a passion for 'Britannias', amongst other things I am sure! His specification was quite simple: it was to be a shed scene and to feature one of the 'Brits' which were fitted with the large BR1D tenders (Bob considered the BR1 tenders fitted to earlier class members to be a little on the small side to visually balance the engine). The rest was up to me! Originally, Leeds Holbeck was to be the location with No. 70053 *Moray Firth* taking centre stage, but eventually Polmadie was chosen, partly as an excuse to feature a 'Duchess' and a 'Scot' and also so that this would allow me to portray No. 70051 *Firth of Forth* (one of my favourites) at home as it were. Built at Crewe in August 1954, No. 70051 went directly to Polmadie where it remained until 1962. A night scene was chosen to heighten drama and focus attention on the lovely lines of these engines which, to a kid growing up in the 1950s, were the last word in modernity. After all, didn't the *Eagle*

comic feature a cutaway drawing in one of those marvellous centre spreads?

'**Shrewsbury Standard**' is a portrait of No. 73003 one of a class of 172 British Railways Standard Class 5s introduced in 1951 and intended to replace various elderly Class 5 4-6-0s throughout the system, although most enginemen preferred their own 'Black 5s', B1s and 'Halls' etc. Despite this time-honoured prejudice they gradually found favour in some parts and did good work, particularly on the Southern. No. 73003 stands by the coaling stage at Shrewsbury shed in 1963 and sports the lined, green passenger livery acquired during a visit to Swindon Works.

A weak but effective light plays upon the stylish lines of another 'Britannia', this time No. 70014 *Iron Duke,* in '**Iron Duke and the Shed Cat**'. Many artists have had a crack at the 'Golden Arrow' but usually with a Bulleid Pacific out on the open road. *Iron Duke* as opposed to

No. 70004 *William Shakespeare,* was chosen because it seems that every article about this famous train features the latter and balance needed to be restored. Before starting this painting I was chatting with a buddy whose brother had been a fireman at Aston shed in Birmingham. When the place closed in 1966 he took home the shed cat which consequently spent its remaining years in a far more presentable state than previously. Its name was Sooty! The 'empty corner' problem was solved again. Reference for Stewarts Lane proved to be plentiful except that I could not find a photograph that included the complete legend on the warehouse in the background. The far left section was the problem. All that could be found was 'MS'. Drifting smoke from the 'King Arthur' solved the quandry. Shortly after the picture was published the perfect photograph was found. 'Strongrooms' proved to be the answer. Sod's Law strikes again!

Firth of Forth (1996)
Oil on Canvas 30" x 24"

Dawn at Dillicar/North Western Style

The West Coast Main Line in the Northern Fells, particularly around Shap, felt familiar long before I actually visited the area. Photographs of 'Duchesses', 'Princesses', 'Scots' and 'Patriots' amongst others pounding to Shap summit leapt from the pages of railway magazines and books. Many of the most beautiful had, of course, been taken by Eric Treacy. Countless others recorded the scene but none quite so effectively as the 'Railway Bishop'. My first 'hands on' experience, probably in 1960, was during a trip with the local locospotters club to Carlisle and points north. Having kept our Friday midnight rendezvous outside the Hall of Memory in Birmingham, 30 or 40 miscreants dozed their way northwards aboard the charabanc dreaming of rare 'Jubes' and 'Scots'. These were pre-M6 Motorway days of course and such journeys seemed endless. It must have been around four in the morning when we made a much-needed stop at a transport cafe near Tebay and afterwards looked in at the station, like you do! No sooner had these zombie like figures set foot upon the platform and peered sleepily along the line when, with a sudden, unexpected rush of cold night air, a southbound express headed by a red 'Coronation' careered past at what seemed hundreds of miles an hour. An extremely eerie and exhilarating sensation. No visible steam or smoke, just a roar and the wheels of the long train clattering over rail joints into the distance. It was all over in seconds. The lasting impression is of a 'Duchess' rocking and swaying wildly towards us and then a crescendo of noise. I realise now, of course, that the train had descended from Shap summit and by the time it reached us would be coasting, yet still going like the wind. This is just one of many visions that must be committed to canvas one of these days!

'**Dawn at Dillicar**' takes us back to an earlier era. As mentioned previously, had I been about in pre-Grouping days I am sure that the London &

North Western Railway would have taken my fancy. They certainly knew how to run a railway, providing the customer with a reliable and punctual service, on the main routes at least. Compared with, for example, a GWR passenger engine the average top-link LNWR locomotive was positively dowdy, to say the least, but what dignity they had! In this painting, commissioned by Mr Richard Willcox, the period is about 1920, the tiny 'Precedent' 2-4-0. popularly known as 'Jumbos', No. 1672 *Talavera* has been relegated from working express trains alone and is being used, very effectively, as pilot to an

Collection: *Private.*

North Western Style (1985)
Oil on Canvas 20" x 16"

almost new 'Claughton' 4-6-0. They are shown skimming over Dillicar troughs, just south of Tebay, in preparation for the charge at Shap bank. The M6 Motorway now dominates the background destroying the once-impressive harmony of railway and landscape.

In '**North Western Style**' an LNWR 'Precursor' 4-4-0, No. 1419 *Tamerlane*, is taking water from Bushey troughs with a Euston–Manchester express c1920. The LNWR was the first railway company to make use of water troughs and eventually had nine sets along the main line between Euston and Carlisle. The engine was designed by George Whale and built at Crewe in March 1904, superheated in 1913 and withdrawn from service by the LMS in March 1936. One hundred and thirty of these excellent machines were built up until August 1907 and typified LNWR locomotive design of this period.

LNWR 'Prince Of Wales'

Dawn at Dillicar (1993)
Oil on Canvas 30" x 24"

St Pancras Departure/Crimson Rambler

Collection: *The Royal Mail.*

Crimson Rambler (1992)
Oil on Canvas 16" x 12"

'**St Pancras Departure**' was inspired by a visit made in 1987 to St Pancras station whilst killing time waiting for a train from King's Cross, just across the road. Gazing at the marvellous roof and feeling a little sad that absolutely nothing was happening in the way of arrivals and departures it occurred to me that the stage was set for the most wonderful railway spectacle but the actors had failed to show. This grim state of affairs was rectified shortly afterwards in my studio – probably to reassure myself that once there was life.

This is an early morning view in the late 1920s with a weak sun bathing the scene with a golden glow which also serves to reduce the marvellous backdrop almost to a monotone silhouette. The angle is carefully chosen so that the shapely towers are placed so as not to 'throw' the composition. The engine, a Compound 4-4-0, No. 1097, has not long emerged brand new from Derby Works under the auspices of the LMS Railway. Built in 1925 it was withdrawn from service as No. 41097 by British Railways in May 1956.

'**Crimson Rambler**' This was a most enjoyable commission to undertake, simply because I was able to work directly from the locomotive at the National Railway Museum at York. The co-operation and courtesy shown to me by the then Head of the Museum, Mr Andrew Dow, made the job a pleasure. A day was spent with No. 1000 at my beck and call positioned on one of the museum's turntables which enabled me to make the necessary drawings for my needs. The engine is shown as it was c1920, stabled around the turntable at Kentish Town shed, London in company with other examples of Midland Railway motive power, including a Kirtley 2-4-0.

Collection: *John Stockton-Wood Esq.*

St Pancras Departure (1987)
Oil on Canvas 20" x 16"

Western Blizzard/Old Oak Winter/Heading South

Collection: *Private.*

Old Oak Winter (1983)
Oil on Board 12" x 10"

Collection: *David Asbury Esq.*

Heading South (1997)
Oil on Canvas 16" x 12"

Only once can I recall being commissioned to paint a railway subject specifically requesting a snow scene. Yet pictures which include this element have been received enthusiastically by publishers and the originals have sold readily. The preference for sunny, summer days is understandable when one considers that many of us recall fondest memories through sun-tinted glasses. Nevertheless, extreme weather conditions offer fascinating possibilities with most subjects and railways are no exception. A favourite combination is sunlight and snow. Hopefully the pictures on these pages make the point.

The poor lineman in '**Western Blizzard**' illustrates that many aspects of work on the railway were sheer purgatory. The figure was in fact my starting point with this painting, with the train taking something of a back seat for a change. A sculptor friend, Keith Lee, was my model and

very patient too, remaining huddled against the storm (on a lovely summer day) for some considerable time whilst the necessary drawings were made. Sunlight is dispersed by the falling snow and heavy impasto passages are evident, particularly in the lower part of the picture, in an attempt to capture the character of freshly fallen snow. The engine, a 'Castle' class 4-6-0, No. 4082 *Windsor Castle*, treads carefully through the south Birmingham suburbs at Acocks Green & South Yardley with a train from Paddington to Wolverhampton during the winter of 1963. At this time I lived in Acocks Green and although most passenger services were dieselised the severe winter saw many duties worked by steam.

In '**Old Oak Winter**' the subjects are illuminated with reverse lighting, that is the visible side of the locomotives are in shade with shadows forming

a vital part of the composition. Advantage is taken of light reflecting off the snow to add interest to shaded areas. The crew of a Stafford Road 'Castle', No. 5063 *Earl Baldwin*, discuss their plight by the coaling stage as one of Old Oak's pannier tanks listens in, c1960.

One of my favourite locomotive types roars through the winter landscape in '**Heading South**' past the lovely, old London & North Western Railway signalbox at Weaver Junction. Beyond is where the Liverpool route leaves the West Coast Main Line. No. 45511 *Isle of Man*, depicted here double-heading a rebuilt 'Royal Scot' in the late 1950s with an up express, was regularly seen in and around Birmingham during my childhood. It was never rebuilt and was withdrawn from service in February 1961.

Western Blizzard (1983)
Oil on Canvas 20" x 16"

North Eastern Elegance/Jersey Lily/Clear Road Through Retford

Collection: *Mr & Mrs D. Barrie.*

North Eastern Elegance (1983)
Oil on Canvas 30" x 24"

Collection: *Richard Martin Esq.*

Jersey Lily (1984)
Oil on Canvas 30" x 20"

This is an excellent example of a subject that would probably never have been painted had I not been asked to. '**North Eastern Elegance**' was commissioned in 1982 by the late Eric Barrie. Eric had spent much of his life living and working in the North East of England and remembered, with great relish, the massive NER Atlantics designed by Sir Vincent Raven and was quite an authority on them. It was fascinating to discuss the pros and cons of the work with him and I learnt a thing or two in the process, including the typical stance of the drivers on these machines. The period is c1920 and the train is leaving Darlington. Eric subsequently asked if I could add the NER coat of arms to the bottom right-hand corner of the painting, which I did, but reluctantly.

Here are two paintings commissioned by Mr Richard Martin of Lichfield. Richard has a passion for Atlantics and has, I believe, built O gauge models of both types seen here. '**Jersey Lily**' is a portrait of a Great Central Class 8B Atlantic designed by J. G. Robinson seen at Neasden shed flanked by a pair of 'Pom-pom' 0-6-0s, at the request of the commissioner. The beautiful livery was quite a challenge to an artist who is more used to depicting rather decrepit, work-worn machines. Richard was brought up in Retford which is on the East Coast Main Line, and wanted a reminder of the lovely Ivatt Atlantics that he just about remembered seeing in his childhood. No. 4444 is speeding across Retford North junction with an up express during the thirties in '**Clear Road Through Retford**'. This picture was used by BR Railfreight in their 1987 calendar where they changed the title to 'East Coast Speed'. Take your pick!

Collection: *Richard Martin Esq.*

Clear Road Through Retford (1983)
Oil on Canvas 30" x 20"

East Coast Elegance

One of the most noteworthy and well documented events on Britain's railways was *Mallard*'s world record breaking high speed exploits when 126 mph was reached at milepost 90¼ on the East Coast Main Line on 3rd July 1938. To commemorate the 50th anniversary of this marvellous achievement I was anxious to produce a painting that was different to those previously seen, and one that really portrayed the elegance, power and speed of Sir Nigel Gresley's A4 Pacifics. Not wishing to show the engine actually breaking the record, this had been done before, I decided on a low viewpoint as one might snatch a glimpse from the line-side. Also it had to be in the condition and livery as on 3rd July 1938, complete with the valance over the wheels and garter blue livery. A feature which always attracts me are those big red driving wheels, partially hidden as if a little shy to display them, like a shy, elegant lady. The composition had to be dynamic, dramatic and appear to

be simple so as to concentrate attention on this beautiful machine at speed.

I ascertained that *Mallard* was at the National Railway Museum and in February 1988 a day was spent sitting on my camera case, gazing at my prey making sketches and taking photographs. A rear three-quarter view was chosen with the A4

No. 4468 'Mallard' approaching Grantham from the north (1938. Drawing made at National Rly Museum York 27. Feb 88

rushing into the canvas. The drawing seen here was made at York with the Grantham elements added later. The approaching A4 is a crafty way of showing the characteristic front-end of these engines but without losing my preferred viewpoint. Grantham was chosen because here there was, and still is, a marvellous, fast, curving approach to the station, far more interesting than a straight run. There was also an attractive signalbox which would make a perfect foil for the on-rushing A4. A suggestion of the shed yard could also be included.

The execution of the work proved to be straightforward and quite brisk in my terms, about eight full days if I remember correctly. The thorough preliminary work proved priceless.

On completion of the painting the erstwhile editor of *Steam Railway* magazine, David Wilcock, chose to feature it on the centre-spread of the July 1988 issue, and Quicksilver Publishing published fine art prints. A satisfactory conclusion!

Collection: *Mike Armstrong Esq.*

East Coast Elegance (1988)
Oil on Canvas 30" x 20"

Cock O' The North

Photo: *Brian Morrison.*

Wood Green
No. 60024 *Kingfisher* on the up 'Tees-Tyne Pullman' – April 1952.

Brian Morrison's OPC book *The Power of the A4s*. I know Brian and phoned him immediately. He confessed that these weren't among his best photographs but would gladly dig out the negatives and make some prints. This he did and kindly sent them within a couple of days. One of them is reproduced here. They provided some good reference for the buildings and layout. Later, more material was discovered, enough to enable me to piece together the total scene. Listening to Eric describing this memorable spectacle was almost as good as being there myself and when work on the canvas began I had acquired a real 'feel' for the task ahead. One of the most rewarding aspects of my work is the ability to recreate someone's fondest memories from way back in the mists of time. I see it as my own, personal 'time machine', not quite as far reaching as that of H. G. Wells, but good enough.

" COCK O' THE NORTH "

When this painting was commissioned by Mr Eric Pearce I was delighted. Nigel Gresley's 'Mikados' had always been a source of fascination. They were rebuilt by his successor Edward Thompson into controversial 'Pacifics' (see 'Night Wolf' earlier), during the war and once again, my only knowledge of the original engines was from photographs in magazines and books. Nevertheless I always felt that No. 2001 looked far more modern than some later designs. Imagine the impression it must have made on small boys, and bigger ones, when it first appeared from Doncaster Works in 1934. Eric was one such small boy and remembers standing on the platforms of his local station, Wood Green on the East Coast Main Line, during the summer of 1934 shortly after the engine was built in May and running trials. In my painting, No. 2001 is passing through Wood Green on one of Eric's fondly remembered summer evenings heading a heavy train towards King's Cross. Shortly after these trials the engine went to France for controlled testing accompanied by Gresley's assistant Mr O. V. S. Bulleid, later of Southern Pacific fame. Whilst in France it was exhibited at the Gare du Nord in Paris.

Reference for Wood Green proved elusive and the only pictures discovered initially were in

Cock O' The North (1988)
Oil on Canvas 30" x 20"

Summit Meeting/Heavy Freight/Citadel Scot

Collection: *Private.*

Heavy Freight (1986)
Oil on Canvas 20" x 16"

Collection: *Private.*

Citadel Scot (1995)
Oil on Canvas 12" x 10"

The 'Crab' 2-6-0, No. 42790, featured in 'Summit Meeting' displays the Saltley trademark of the time (c1960) of a clean, black smokebox (actually a liberal coating of grease). The painting was commissioned by Mr Paul Freer who lives a few miles north of here, next to the line, at Barnt Green. The famous Lickey incline climbs for two miles from Bromsgrove to Blackwell, (this view is from the platform at the latter), at a gradient of 1 in 37 was, and still is I believe, the steepest continuous stretch of main line in the country. Here, at the summit, a southbound freight grinds to a halt to enable wagon brakes to be pinned down – one of the many regulations imposed upon trains descending the incline. Battling up the grade with a passenger service from Bristol is a Barrow Road 'Jubilee', No. 45699 *Galatea*, a regular on this route during the late 1950s and early '60s. It was one of the unfortunates slandered as a 'crate' in New Street station but also happened to be one of the fortunate few that found its way to Barry scrapyard when withdrawn in 1964 and, at the time of writing, is a kit of rusty parts at the Birmingham Railway Museum, Tyseley. The 'Lickey' was a wonderful place to watch locomotives hard at work and indeed, was heavily populated with train watchers of all ages at weekends and holidays during steam days.

In the 1950s we saw a few 9Fs on the Western lines at home but later Saltley shed was discovered where many of them lived. In 'Heavy Freight' No. 92118, one of the Saltley fleet, is getting under way with a heavy train of iron-ore and viewed from the disused platforms of Saltley station in the early 1960s. Ahead lies the steep climb to Camp Hill (see also 'Bordesley Meeting') and a hard slog for the fireman. I have tried to make the most of the contrast of a sunny day and filthy engine topped off by the volcanic eruptions from the chimney. Exhausts such as this always remind me of a caption to a photograph by Eric Treacy when he described an A3 as 'talking to the sky' – must use that one of these days! In the background lurk two of Birmingham's beauty spots, Nechells Power Station and Washwood Heath Gasworks. The aroma was intoxicating!

Carlisle Citadel (they don't name them like that anymore) station became well trodden during the early 1960s particularly during the wee small hours awaiting connections to here and there. In 'Citadel Scot' the purposeful form of rebuilt 'Royal Scot', No. 46125 *3rd Carabinier*, catches the sunlight struggling through the smokey atmosphere as it awaits departure time with a Glasgow–Birmingham express in the early 1960s.

Collection: *Paul Freer Esq.*

Summit Meeting (1994)
Oil on Canvas 30" x 24"

Low Level Departure/Home From the Seaside/View From a Bridge

Collection: *Charles Pagett Esq.*

Home From the Seaside (1986)
Oil on Canvas 30" x 20"

Collection: *David Reynolds Esq.*

View From A Bridge (1996)
Oil on Canvas 30" x 20"

The reader will be aware by now that I saw a lot of the 'Cornishman', indeed from 1960 until 1962 hardly a day passed that did not find me, when the evenings were light enough, perched upon my bicycle saddle propped against Tyseley bridge, glancing at my watch impatient for six-thirty to arrive when this magnificent spectacle would ease into view, if running to time. However, at this stage of the long journey, having left Penzance at 10.30 in the morning, it was usually behind schedule. David Asbury also saw a lot of this train but at Wolverhampton Low Level station during the 1950s. A Stafford Road 'County' would often be the motive power and fittingly, No. 1004 *County of Somerset* is depicted here in '**Low Level Departure**', in BR lined black livery in original single-chimney condition carrying the original pattern headboard. Departure from Low Level was at 9.15 in the morning and relief trains would also run on summer Saturdays, both before and after the main train. The other protagonists are a Hawksworth pannier tank, No. 8411, and Churchward Prairie

tank No. 5151, both allocated to 84A at this time. The pannier is engaged on station pilot duties and the Prairie is waiting in the up bay platform with a Stourbridge local. The contraption fitted to the smokebox of No. 1004 is a reporting number frame which should carry the number 825. Presumably shed staff at 84A did not have the numbers to hand or no time to fit them. This characteristic Great Western accessory can be seen in other paintings in this collection, both full and empty!

'**Home From the Seaside**' features the northbound train climbing away from Stratford upon Avon approaching Danzey on the North Warwickshire line c1960. Commissioned by Mr Charles Pagett who, on regular family visits during the 1950s to his uncle who lived near to the orchard shown on the right of the picture, would spend hours watching the trains at this location. The engine is a Stafford Road 'Castle', No. 5063 *Earl Baldwin,* showing off the later decorative headboard complete with Cornish

piskey leapfrogging over a toadstool!

Whilst discussing what was to become '**View From a Bridge**' with Mr David Reynolds who commissioned the picture, I discovered that he too had spent hours on Tyseley bridge but during the early to mid 1950s, a little earlier than I. His favourite 'Castle' was No. 5031 *Totnes Castle*, another Stafford Road regular. The 'Cornishman' at this time was often made up of Hawksworth stock in BR carmine and cream livery (blood and custard to us) and is seen coming off the North Warwick line to join the down relief on the main Paddington–Birmingham route. After cautiously passing through Tyseley it will join the down main before calling at Birmingham Snow Hill and eventually journey's end at Wolverhampton Low Level. A Tyseley 'matchbox' fusses with wagons on the shunting spur next to the up main. This view is still recognisable today including the terraced houses although the track layout has been rationalised during the intervening years and of course, the signalbox and signals have long gone.

Low Level Departure (1997)
Oil on Canvas 30" x 24"

Exeter St Davids/Evening at Yardley Wood/The Power and the Glory

Collection: *David Antley Esq.*

Evening at Yardley Wood (1993)
Oil on Canvas 30" x 24"

Collection: *Colin Washbourne Esq.*

The Power and the Glory (1991)
Oil on Canvas 30" x 24"

A fine art print of '**Exeter St Davids**' was published in 1994 and launched at the Exeter Rail Fair in that year. It was later realised that the headlamps on *King John* had no handles. Some weeks later I rectified the omission on the original painting and took the opportunity to alter one or two other things including the addition of a driver leaning from the cab. The version seen here is the latter – complete with headlamp handles! The painting depicts the late 1950s, perhaps 1959 when I first discovered St Davids as referred to in Chapter 3 (Holidays and Trains), the footbridge is the very one from which the noisy 'Warship' was witnessed. 'King' class 4-6-0 No. 6026 *King John* sweeps majestically through the centre road in charge of the down 'Cornish Riviera Express' complete with decorative headboard and reporting numbers.

Prairie tank No. 4117 waits to follow with a stopping train for Newton Abbot while 'West Country' No. 34023 *Blackmore Vale* waits for a path to Exeter Central with a train from Plymouth. The building in the background is the same one seen in 'Night Freight', reproduced earlier in this book.

'**Evening at Yardley Wood**' shows the northbound 'Cornishman' passing through the Birmingham suburbs at Yardley Wood in 1960. My brief from Mr Dave Antley who commissioned the work, was straightforward. As a kid he had spent time on the road bridge, which also served as a footbridge, to watch this train, just as I did three stations along the line at Tyseley. I had some photographic reference taken in the 1970s when the station still appeared

much has it had since between the wars, including the lamps, nameboards and platform awnings. There would be a problem with the platform hiding the wheels of the engine, but with some careful juggling of the angles this was overcome. Before a start was made on the canvas a visit was made to the station – still open and well used but much of the paraphernalia of a real railway, the old lamps and nameboards had been replaced with modern functional but heartless substitutes. The platform awnings had also been replaced with perspex sheets. The locomotive incidently, is 'Castle' No. 5072 *Hurricane*.

'**The Power and the Glory**' was commissioned by Mr Colin Washbourne, a member of the 6024 Preservation Society, as a reward for himself having grafted for years on the restoration of the

Collection: *Ron King Esq.*

Exeter St Davids (1994)
Oil on Canvas 30" x 20"

engine, first at Quainton Road and then at Didcot. He specifically wanted the painting to portray 'his' engine in Great Western days. This necessitated having to un-rebuild the 'King' with a single chimney, straight steam pipes and so on.

Also it had to be working hard, and as *King Edward I* was a West Country resident during the chosen period, 1947, we decided on Dainton bank as the location, as it would have worked between Paddington and Plymouth almost

exclusively. Ample reference material was at hand having visited the area frequently over the years. The scene is what many would consider to be the epitome of all that was great about the Great Western.

Sunshine and Steam

Early in 1987 I received a letter from the BBC asking if I would accept a commission for a painting with a 'West Country' flavour that could be published as a fine art print. A

recent years too and was aware that the semaphore signal, railings and practically everything else was still as I knew it in the '50s including, of course, the distinctive red sandstone

cliffs. In fact the only noticeable difference, apart from the motive power, was that the footbridge had been replaced by a modern concrete structure. Since 1987 colour-light signalling has replaced the semaphores along this route.

Once again, my son Ben stood in for me and the figure groups are taken from family snapshots of the period, and the locomotive chosen was No. 6023 *King Edward II* which, at this time, was a 'kit of parts' languishing in the 'fish bay' at Bristol Temple Meads. It has since been transferred to the Great Western Society at Didcot where restoration work is currently in progress.

The finished work was well received by the BBC and following some excellent television, radio and press coverage, the prints sold extremely well and raised several pounds for 'Children In Need'.

Canvas size
30" x 20"

Double chimney
'King' heading
the 'up' 'Cornish
Riviera', 1954.

Left: A composition which was rejected. The angle made me feel uncomfortable – sitting on those spiked railings!

DAWLISH PROM' – 1958.

proportion of the proceedings from each print sold would be donated to the 'Children In Need' fund later in the year. Obviously, I was delighted and, upon inquiring further, realised that I was to have a completely free hand regarding the subject and location. The only criteria was that it should appeal to a wide audience and not only railway enthusiasts. I drifted back immediately to summer holidays with my parents in the 1950s and standing transfixed to the railings on the promenade at Dawlish in Devon watching the trains go by. The attractive headboards proclaiming the passage of the 'Torbay Express', the 'Mayflower', the 'Cornishman', the 'Royal Duchy' and the 'Cornish Riviera Express' remain etched in my memory bank. To extend the West Country theme I chose to portray the 'Cornish Riviera Express'. I knew the location well from

Right: This is the angle finally selected. I preferred the lower viewpoint which I feel adds a certain dignity to the locomotive and allows the viewer to feel more comfortable on the 'right' side of the fence.

DAWLISH PROM – '58

Collection: *BBC Radio Devon.*

Sunshine and Steam (1987)
Oil on Canvas 30" x 20"

Approaching Solihull/Lyme Regis Bound/Great Western Style

Collection: *Ron & Freda Cass.*

Approaching Solihull (1986)
Oil on Board 12" x 10"

Collection: *Ron & Freda Cass.*

Lyme Regis Bound (1987)
Oil on Canvas 20" x 16"

These three paintings belong to my 'cow parsley' period. This plant, as I'm sure you know, has 'umbrellas' of tiny white flowers and is prolific on railway embankments, and practically everywhere else, during May and June and I became quite enamoured for a while, taking photographs and making sketches with a view to incorporating them in paintings, when appropriate of course. The paintings are also examples of the type of scene that is most often requested by would-be clients. They are straightforward front three-quarter views of trains in a sylvan setting. Perhaps the popular idea of a 'railway painting'. My own preference is for more urban or industrial surroundings, but I can well understand the popularity of the open countryside of course, and enjoy such paintings, especially when they 'work'. An added bonus too

"GREAT WESTERN STYLE"

is that the amount of reference involved is usually less than for a busy station scene, for example.

'**Approaching Solihull**' portrays a 'King' heading the 8.33am Wolverhampton–Paddington express viewed from Streetsbrook Road bridge in 1962 on the four-track main line out of Birmingham. This was a train I saw hundreds of times both when living in Winson Green and later in Acocks Green and was invariably a 'King' job until the end of the summer 1962 when these majestic engines were replaced by the new 'Western' diesel-hydraulics. Many years later, in the 1970s, I was to photograph many 'Westerns' from this same bridge.

'**Lyme Regis Bound**' is an idyllic scene, in the fifties, on the 7-mile long branch line to Lyme

78

Great Western Style (1986)
Oil on Canvas 30" x 20"

Regis, which left the ex London & South Western Railway's main line at Axminster. No. 30583 was one of three Adams radial tanks that were retained to work this unusually difficult and twisting line. They proved to be ideally suited to these conditions and were synonymous with this service until 1961. They became something of an anachronism and attracted enthusiasts from far and wide. In my picture the engine wears British Railways lined black livery, which suited it well I think. It has now been preserved for more than 30 years on the Bluebell Railway.

'**Great Western Style**' was the ideal commission. The instructions went something like this – 'A Great Western express train speeding along the open road on a sunny, summer day between the wars'. What more could I ask for? Here was an excuse to paint a 'Saint'. Lovely engines, which make me wish that I had been born earlier. What a pity that none are preserved. The period is the 'roaring twenties' with an up express tearing out of Sonning cutting near Reading, headed by No. 2922 *Saint Gabriel*.

Sonning Cutting/The 'Inter-City'

Collection: *Private.*

Sonning Cutting (1984)
Oil on Canvas 14" x 10"

As railway cuttings go Sonning must surely be the most famous. The excellent and much published photographs by the late Maurice Earley have made it familiar to all railway enthusiasts. Brunel's planned route for the Great Western Railway's first broad gauge main line from Paddington to Bristol dictated that his civil engineers had to excavate this long, wide, deep and very impressive cutting on the approach to Reading. Just imagine the manpower required for such an undertaking in those premechanised days. During the steam era there was an almost constant procession of traffic along this very busy main line. In '**Sonning Cutting**' No. 6024 *King Edward I* is heading a down express in the late fifties. 'The Power and the Glory', featured previously, shows this engine at an earlier stage in its career.

The period in '**The Inter-City**' is the same as the previous picture and was commissioned by Mr Charles Pagett, who now lives near the south end of this station, Knowle & Dorridge. The 'Inter-City' was a regular 'King' turn, although 'Castles' were used on occasion. The engine is No. 6013 *King Henry VIII*. Just left, beyond the shops, is the Dorridge Gallery where many of my paintings have been framed over the years, and along Station Approach to the right is an off-licence which dad used to manage.

Collection: *Charles Pagett Esq.*

The 'Inter-City' (1989)
Oil on Canvas 30" x 20"

The Bristolian

In 1987 the Bristol United Press newspaper group commissioned a painting to celebrate the naming of an HST power car after the company. The subject chosen, after several interesting meetings, was appropriately, the steam hauled 'Bristolian'. During BR days this train carried a very attractive headboard that incorporated the coats of arms of both London and Bristol. This would feature strongly in the painting as would the beautiful, sweeping arch of the roof at Temple Meads station. Also, I wanted to introduce an element that would indicate the importance of Bristol as an inter-regional crossroads. The West of England to the North services were very busy in the 1950s, particularly during the summer months. One of these trains had to be included in the picture. The year was to be 1959 and July of that year saw the 'Warship' diesel-hydraulics taking over the 'Bristolian' from the 'Castles'. I chose to depict this final phase of steam haulage.

Technically, the picture is rather complex because of the curve of the tracks and consequently the roof called for some careful calculations. Several visits were made to sketch and photograph details of the view required. Unfortunately the viewpoint

cream, discoloured, stains etc
Detail of platform canopy awning

Pigeons perhaps on roof.

in my painting is now ruined by the ugly Royal Mail parcels bridge at the London end of the platforms. Train spotters were a constant feature here, as at many large stations, and they made full use of any available seating. To this end I found some typical Great Western parcels trollies on the Torbay Steam Railway in Devon and duly used these to seat the aforementioned 'spotters' who would be noting down details of their latest 'cops'. The inclusion of such detail is, I feel, vital to the overall impact and also serves to add scale and a certain majesty to the locomotives and the imposing surroundings. Another important touch is the inclusion of one of the ubiquitous pannier tanks on the centre road. This provides an ideal contrast with the two passenger engines. The ever-present 'station' pigeons complete the scene.

The finished painting was unveiled in the newspaper's boardroom in front of several British Rail officials. Later, I was invited, along with the congregation, to witness a naming ceremony at Temple Meads where the nameplates *Bristol Evening Post* were unveiled on HST power car No. 43150 in October 1988.

Late 50's period 9:30 pm

'Castle' class loco with ornate headboard.

LNER 'Jubilee' on left

Busy platform including train-spotters.

Trolleys.

light from rest of roof

The Bristolian @ Temple Meads (Platform 9 & 10)

30" × 24" canvas

Shorten hair - 50's style

'Ben' Aug '88

'Train-spotter' to sit on trolley with note book etc.

Light

'Patriot' No. 45509 at far platform. Substitute for 'Jubilee'.

Metal

Black (battered)

Brown

Luggage trolley sketched @ Kingswear. Aug '88.

'Train-spotter' to sit on trolley - 2nd figure.

The Bristolian (1988)
Oil on Canvas 30" x 24"

Preparing for Nightfall/Black 5 at Bristol

Preparing for Nightfall (1991)
Oil on Board 12" x 10"

making a rare visit north of the border. I knew this engine well during the fifties when it was a Bushbury resident and a regular on 'my bank' and at New Street.

When Mr John Petcher commissioned '**Black 5 at Bristol**' he specifically stated that he wanted a painting of a 'Black 5' and a Compound on shed in LMS days. I enjoy shed scenes, perhaps because the ever-present muck and clutter gives plenty of scope to improvise. The larger Midland Railway shed buildings are attractive and Bristol Barrow Road was chosen because of the amount of reference available. Several of the larger MR sheds shared the same architectural features. Holbeck and Burton, for example, are very similar to this. Great care has to be taken when portraying 'Black 5s'. There are many design and detail variations to trap the unwary. Research revealed that No. 5293, an example from the Armstrong Whitworth factory built in 1936, was a Bristol (22A) engine in 1938, the year in question. At the same time Compound No. 1123 was a Saltley (21A) engine and a regular visitor to Barrow Road. So, I had the actors, and most of the information needed to complete the stage.

The 'Black 5' had to be the main protagonist with No. 1123 in a supporting role. The contrasting liveries had artistic potential and would serve to lift the otherwise sombre tones. Again, the figures are important to add scale and a human presence. The 'banter' between the enginemen helps to make the composition flow. Smoke and steam are kept to a minimum. There is a tendency to overdo this aspect of shed scenes, but in this case I feel that the understatement is more effective. The inspection pit is important and allows the viewer to wander into the picture and 'mooch' around.

Sir William Stanier's engines loomed large in my childhood. 'Black 5s', 'Jubilees' and rebuilt 'Scots' were almost a part of the family. I loved the names, particularly those of the 'Jubilees'. As mentioned elsewhere, I was able to answer some unusual general knowledge questions at school thanks to the 'Jubes'.

'**Preparing for Nightfall**' features 'Jubilee' No. 45733 *Novelty* and 'Black 5' No. 44674 at Polmadie shed, Glasgow in 1963. The shed lights, such as they are, begin to take over from daylight as the engines are prepared for duty. *Novelty* wears a 2A shedplate indicating that its home shed was Rugby, many miles south, and is

Collection: *John Petcher Esq.*

Black 5 at Bristol (1983)
Oil on Canvas 30" x 20"

Newton Heath Morning

Whenever possible I use my own photographs as a source of reference but rarely is the final painting based so entirely on these as 'Newton Heath Morning'.

Reproduced here are photographs taken on a very dull and gloomy Sunday morning in July 1964. With most unusual foresight I realised the potential of a wide shot. As this could not be encompassed within a single exposure I actually took two from exactly the same position with a view to joining them together later. Sadly this is an isolated example of forward planning but it paid dividends some six or seven years later when I made a water colour painting based on this reference. I vaguely remember being rather pleased with the result and sold it soon afterwards. Not one detail of the transaction was noted and consequently I have not seen the painting from that day to this.

Quite by chance, some 17 years later, whilst searching for some quite different London, Midland reference, I came across the two postcard sized photographs still taped together in an ancient Kodak box. The shed setting was exactly what I was looking for at the time and there seemed little point in hunting further. It will be noticed from the finished work that weather conditions have improved drastically over the intervening 23 years and human life has been added to the scene by including the engineman. Carefully planned lighting, smoke, steam and shadows mingle to recreate an evocative memory, to me at least, of a typical shed-bashing trip of more than 30 years ago, and absolutely authentic – except the weather. This was a particularly rewarding project, not least because every scrap of information had been gathered by me including the list of numbers seen at Newton Heath on, just another day in 1964.

Top, right: *The relevant page from author's notebook, 1964.*
Below: *'Royal Scot' No. 46140 The King's Royal Rifle Corps at Newton Heath.*
Below, right: *'Jinty' 0-6-0T No. 47582 at Newton Heath.*

Collection: *John Hobbs Esq.*

Newton Heath Morning (1987)
Oil on Canvas 20" x 16"

Unsung Hero

Handwritten annotations on the sketch:

YORK SHED YARD - LOOKING, SOUTH-EAST, TICORAINS LOCO in workaday condition - filthy! rust stains etc.

LOW BACK/SIDE LIGHT

Smokey atmosphere

ECML in left background

WD behind 63601

'A1' Pacific in background - maybe!

Coal tower in background poles etc figures.

debris etc on ground

Perhaps 30"×26" canvas on scene props.

"UNSUNG HERO"

63601 @ YORK MPD 1950's

goodness sake! No. 63601 in ex-works condition just did not appeal – it had to be liberally coated in work-stained glory. The WD coupled up behind was an obvious choice, the two types seem so well matched. By way of contrast, and to illustrate that York shed entertained both freight and passenger locomotives, is the inclusion of an A4 Pacific, No. 60015 *Quicksilver* (you have to keep publishers happy) and A1 No. 60154 *Bon Accord*. The period is c1960.

It will be noticed that the composition was lowered within the picture area and the decision made during work on the canvas to darken the mood – I wanted a more intimate atmosphere.

A page from one of the author's notebooks, complete with No. 63601, 16th June 1963.

Freight locomotives have cast a spell since the constant parade of 4Fs and 'Super Ds' passed my home as a child. The unglamorous, workaday nature of these grime-covered machines was hard to resist. My first encounter with the O4s was during 1959 on a day out to Doncaster aboard a special train hauled by Compound 1000. Mexborough shed was included in the itinerary and it seemed, to this 11-year old, to consist of 'wall to wall' O4s and WDs, all in absolutely filthy condition. Later visits were made to such beauty spots as Staveley, Retford and Frodingham and so on. With all this in the memory bank, when *Steam Railway* magazine launched a campaign to raise funds for the restoration of No. 63601 in the National Collection, it seemed quite natural to get involved. Quicksilver Publishing would produce a high quality, very limited edition fine art print with almost 20 per cent of the purchase price donated to the 'O4 Fund'. After meetings with

representatives of the magazine, including Managing Editor Nigel Harris, a strategy was resolved with the original painting to be the prize for the lucky winner of a special *Steam Railway* competition. Perhaps the winner is reading this – 'hello!'. The December 1997 edition carried a feature on 'yours truly' and the preparation of '**Unsung Hero**', followed in the January issue by the launch of the limited edition print.

York shed yard was chosen as the location because, as a Frodingham engine, No. 63601 would have been a regular visitor with freight for one of the many yards around York, and adjourned to the shed for servicing. This, plus the fact that on withdrawal in June 1963 for preservation, it had spent many years at the York museum, amongst other places, pending restoration. Who would have thought that it would take well over 30 years? The engines in the National Collection belong to us all for

Unsung Hero (1997)
Oil on Canvas 30" x 20"

Twilight of the Fifties

By the summer of 1991 only a handful of Class 50s were still in service and even those were not expected to see the year out. Quicksilver Publishing was keen to commemorate their passing with the issue of a fine art print. Hence the creation of 'Twilight of the Fifties'.

My immediate thoughts turned to Laira, Plymouth, a depot which had a long association with these diesel-electrics, with the idea of producing a painting of them 'on shed', and to take the opportunity of working from 'life'. Consequently, during May contact was made with British Rail in the person of Geoff Hudson, Area Fleet Manager at Laira. His reaction was very encouraging and after clearance with various departments of BR arrangements were made for me to visit the depot in June. After donning a look-out vest and prowling around for an hour or two, several options had come to mind. What I had pictured was a 'busy' scene inside the maintenance shop with more than one Class 50 in view. Several ideas were discussed with my minders

and the remainder of the day was spent making sketches and taking photographs. Armed with this reference I adjourned to my studio, refined my thoughts and produced the drawing shown here. A copy was sent to Laira to ascertain from Geoff whether or not the scenario could be staged for a second visit, which had to be quite soon to give sufficient time to complete the painting. His reaction was prompt and very enthusiastic. True to his word, and much to my

50002 - LAIRA MAINTAINANCE DEPOT
from reference taken - 6ᵗʰ June 1991

delight, July saw me once again in Devon and as I peered through the maintenance shop door the envisaged picture was there to greet me. The locomotive on the jacks was No. 50048 *Dauntless* with sister engines hovering about which I could arrange to have positioned wherever required.

On being confronted with this enticing spectacle I immediately decided to change my original viewpoint and several other details were altered. Two of Laira's 'B' shift fitters, Mike Collings and Clive Young, entered into the spirit of things when recruited as models and showed great restraint whilst sketches were made. A most enjoyable day made possible by the friendly co-operation and enthusiasm of Geoff Hudson and his staff.

The whole exercise was rounded off by the launch of the print at the Laira open day in September where I spent the day signing copies. A very satisfactory conclusion to five months' work and a real treat to have all the necessary information at my finger tips rather than relying on historical reference.

Collection: *Artist's.*

Twilight of the Fifties (1991)
Oil on Canvas 30" x 20"

Twilight of the Twenties

To continue the 'Twilight' theme and the success of the Class 50 project of the previous year, the same publisher was anxious to follow up with a print issue for 1992. The Class 20s presented themselves as perfect candidates. Only a handful of these popular diesels remained in normal service having been an integral part of the British railway scene for 35 years, far longer than intended.

As with the 50s, I was determined to work from 'life' and after several abortive attempts to arrange visits to Toton depot and continually banging my head against British Rail red tape, attention turned closer to home, at Bescot. The response to my initial calls was positive and it soon became clear that the Bescot lads would be willing and able to help with my task. Arrangements were made by the West Midlands Area Freight Manager, Les McDowell, and at 8 o'clock on a very warm June evening I presented myself at the depot to be met by driver Tony Bill who had volunteered to be my guide. Sketches of my intentions had already been made. Ideally my painting was to be a night scene with a pair of Class 20s leaving the yard with a coal train and my immediate task was to find the location

where this scenario could take place. The next two or three hours were spent stalking the marshalling yards with Tony feeding me invaluable information regarding the workings of the yard and details of signalling, amongst other things. Eventually the ideal place was found. At the north end of the down yard, adjacent to the diesel depot, was exactly what I envisaged, right down to the signal which was to

LIGHT PYLON

be a crucial part of the composition. Tony even phoned the power box to ask if the coloured light could be changed to the aspect seen in the painting. His request was declined when it was explained that repercussions would be felt for

several miles along the line! The required sketches were made and photographs were taken with the only thing missing being the locomotives.

One of the trains that had departed the yards at the location in question was a merry-go-round service to Ironbridge Power Station. Until a year or two previously Class 20s had been in charge – perfect. More research revealed that several 20s had been based at Bescot including No. 20160 which, although withdrawn in December 1990, was still stored elsewhere in the yards. More sketches and photographs followed. By 3 o'clock in the morning I had sufficient reference to make a start. Tony had been patience personified and a mine of information too.

As at Laira it was very satisfying to work with informed and enthusiastic BR men and Les McDowell and Tony Bill were certainly that.

The prints were launched at Bescot open day on 30th August where my painting was actually duplicated in the yard beside the depot, even to the extent that a Class 37 was positioned exactly as in the picture. The only details missing were the snowploughs! The painting was used on the cover of the open day programme and also reproduced in several magazines at this time.

Twilight of the Twenties (1992)
Oil on Panel 24" x 18"

North Pole Dawn/Docklands – Then and Now

Docklands – Then and Now (1994)
Oil on Canvas 30" x 20"

For the most part I graft away in the studio surrounded with reference books, photographs, maps, timetables, notes, drawings, anything that may be of use with the work in hand. You get the picture! Sometimes a breath of fresh air arrives when asked to portray a contemporary subject. These pages illustrate two such cases. Both were commissioned quite out of the blue and unconnected early in 1994, both involved frequent trips to London, initially discussion meetings and later, reference gathering. '**North Pole Dawn**' was commissioned by European Passenger Services to celebrate the imminent launch of 'Eurostar' services to the Continent through the Channel Tunnel. A

meeting was arranged at the newly opened North Pole depot in London and after satisfying the gathering that I could come up with the goods, plans were made to make a start. Initially sketches were prepared to ensure that we were all on the same wave length and then some in depth research work was carried out. Mr Stuart Whitter, EPS Fleet Engineering Manager, arranged several visits to North Pole where 'Eurostar' units were placed at my disposal and positioned as required. Stuart's enthusiastic co-operation made for a most enjoyable project resulting in fine art prints of the painting being presented to all members of staff at a presentation at the depot towards the end of the year in

recognition of their tremendous efforts – a lovely touch and one which was much appreciated.

'**Docklands – Then and Now**' was commissioned by Brown & Root, Booz . Allen Ltd, main contractors for the Docklands Light Railway. During our initial meeting at their London headquarters in Docklands I suggested the idea of combining the old and new as an evocation of the vast changes and regeneration of the area in recent years and, of course, featuring the railway. After several interesting meetings a pass, issued for the Docklands Light Railway system, was extensively used during the following weeks to gather reference for the main subject. Several

Collection: *European Passenger Services.*

North Pole Dawn (1994)
Oil on Canvas 30" x 20"

visits to the Docklands Archive in Poplar for historic material threw up information on the various docks in the area. This information enabled a start to be made on the canvas. All in all a most enjoyable exercise. A limited edition print and greetings cards were published by Quicksilver Publishing for internal circulation throughout the company. It's not all steam you know!

Index